Dad,

Happy Father's Day! 1997.

From,

Laura & Christian & Rebecca

xxx.

THE ESSENTIALS OF JAPANESE COOKING

Tokiko Suzuki

SHUFUNOTOMO /
JAPAN PUBLICATIONS

First printing, 1995

© Copyright in Japan 1994 by Tokiko Suzuki
Photographs by Takehiko Takei
Book Design by Momoyo Nishimura

Published by SHUFUNOTOMO CO., LTD.
2-9, Kanda Surugadai, Chiyoda-ku, Tokyo, 101 Japan

DISTRIBUTORS
United States: Kodansha America, Inc., through Farrar, Straus &
Giroux, 19 Union Square West, New York, NY 10003.
Canada: Fitzhenry & Whiteside Ltd., 195 Allstate Parkway, Markham,
Ontario L3R 4T8.
British Isles and European Continent: Premier Book Marketing Ltd.,
1 Gower Street, London WC1E 6HA, United Kingdom.
Australia and New Zealand: Bookwise International, 54 Crittenden
Road, Findon, South Australia 5023.
The Far East and Japan: Japan Publications Trading Co., Ltd.,
1-2-1, Sarugaku-cho, Chiyoda-ku, Tokyo 101, Japan

ISBN: 0-87040-950-6
Printed in Japan

PREFACE

Japan, a nation of long, narrow, and mountainous islands, owes her unique cuisine to her geography. From these mountains and seas come the seafood, seaweeds, mountain vegetables and mushrooms which make up a diet widely recognized for its low fat content.

The Japanese people treasure the beauty and dynamism of nature with its four distinct seasons. This is evident in the cuisine, which takes advantage of the various foods available at each time of the year to create an ever-changing menu of tastes and combinations.

When we prepare dishes in the spring, we employ bright colors and a light atmosphere to connote blossoming flowers and budding leaves. Cool, refreshing accents are added to dishes and to table settings during the heat and humidity of summer. The onset of autumn warrants a quiet, peaceful dining atmosphere, with dishes and settings reflecting the burnished colors of autumn leaves in the mountains and reminding us of the harvest season. The cold winter is heralded by an abundance of prime ocean fare, which is prepared as sashimi or cooked in one-pot dishes to preserve the freshness that is the essence of Japanese cooking.

Chosen from such a diverse range, the dishes in this collection are easy to make, healthy and ever popular. I hope this book finds a permanent niche in your kitchen library.

Tohiko Suzuki

CONTENTS

Metric Conversion Table

1 oz. = 30 grams	1 teaspoon = 5 ml
1 lb. = 0.45 kg	1 tablespoon = 15 ml
1 fluid oz. = 30 ml	1″ = 2.5 cm
1 cup = 0.24 liters	

◆ All recipes serve four persons unless otherwise stated.
◆ Numbers in paarentheses refer to color plates.

The Principles of Japanese Cuisine

Maximizing Natural Flavors, Colors and Textures

Most Japanese cuisine is seasoned only lightly; strong spices are rarely used. Although this may initially seem bland to a Western palate, the Japanese believe this allows the true flavors of foods to come through.

Sashimi best exemplifies this principle. Rather than cook fresh fish with heavy oils, herbs or spices, Japanese generally prefer to savor its natural flavor and freshness.

The same is true of vegetables. Spinach or green beans, for example, are only lightly cooked and seasoned to preserve their texture and flavor.

Echoing the Seasons

Although nowadays we are able to procure almost any ingredient at any time of year, Japanese cuisine still changes with the seasons. Each season is celebrated with special dishes. Rice with Fresh Green Peas, for example, is a summer dish, while Harvest Rice, with its freshly harvested rice and mushrooms, heralds the onset of fall.

Not only do ingredients change with the seasons, but there is also seasonal variation in cooking methods, even in garnishes. Sprigs of *kinome* signify springtime; green *shiso* and ginger appear in the summer; while *yuzu* citron peel and *mitsuba* are fall and winter garnishes.

Using seasonal ingredients may seem old-fashioned, but, if for no other reason, it offers the freshest ingredients at their peak—and at their best prices!

Healthy Ingredients and Cooking Methods

Japanese cuisine is well-known for its healthy ingredients: fish, vegetables, seaweeds and soy bean products. Even when it comes to stock, while Western cuisine uses meat bouillon, Japanese stock consists only of dried fish and seaweed.

When compared to the use of oil, say, in Chinese cooking, Japanese cuisine is often termed a "water-based cuisine." Apart from the few deep-fried dishes in this book, most contain no oil at all. Dressings are made with dashi, not oil. Indeed, even such fried foods as *aburage* and meatballs are rinsed with water before serving to eliminate excess oil.

Japanese food is thus especially good for those concerned about their weight, their heart or their cholesterol levels.

Planning a Japanese Meal

A Japanese meal is made up of several dishes, each using a different cooking method. Generally, a meal will consist of one soup and two or three dishes: a salad, a grilled dish, a fried dish or, perhaps, a simmered dish. When grilled fish is served as the main dish, for example, a salad or simmered vegetable or tofu will be served on the side. If one dish is especially rich or filling—a chunky soup, sushi or a *nabe* (one-pot) dish—then the side dishes are either reduced in number or kept simple. Such careful matching of dishes ensures that flavors and textures complement each other and that the meal is nutritionally balanced.

Still eaten up to three times a day by some Japanese, rice is the best complement to Japanese dishes. Rice and pickles are usually served with the dishes, while green tea and fruits or candies may follow. Desserts do not, however, play a major part in Japanese cuisine.

When preparing a meal for guests, serve saké together with an appetizer which complements it. (As saké is rice-based, it is never served with or after rice.) Also, instead of just increasing the quantities of a dish, increase the number of dishes served.

Meals celebrating seasonal events or festivals have appropriately themed menus to enhance the festive mood.

Ingredients

If you have trouble finding some of the ingredients for recipes, try taking this book along to Oriental food-stores to match up the photographs, or to show to the store owner. As far as possible, substitutes are suggested. For other ingredients such as tofu, *nori* or *wasabi*, for example, there is no substitute.

The difference between Oriental and Western vegetables is greater than it initially seems. Even familiar-sounding vegetables, such as Japanese spinach, cucumbers, egg-plants, peppers, leeks and sweet potatoes, are smaller and often sweeter than their Western relatives. Nevertheless, for all the recipes in this book, the latter is fine.

Vegetables, Mushrooms and Nuts

1. Lotus Roots
2. *Daikon* Sprouts
    (*Kaiware-na*)
3. *Seri*
4. *Negi, Wakegi*
5. Sweet Potatoes
6. *Shishi-togarashi* Peppers
7. *Shungiku*
8. Burdock
    (*Gobo*)
9. Mushrooms (from left to right: *Shiitake, Shimeji, Enoki* mush-rooms)
10. Baby Cucumbers
    (*Morokyu*)
11. *Komatsu-na*
12. *Daikon* Radish
13. Gingko Nuts
14. *Udo*

Herbs and Edible Flowers

1. *Wasabi*
2. Green *Shiso*
   (*Ao-jiso*)
3. *Mitsuba*
4. *Yuzu* Citron
5. Ginger
6. Shiso Seed Pods
   (*Hana-ho-jiso*)
7. *Me-negi*
8. *Sudachi*
9. *Myoga* Shoots

10. *Shiso* Sprouts
    (*Me-jiso*)
11. *Asatsuki*
12. Yellow Chrysanthemum Flowers
13. *Kinome*
14. *Beni-tade*
15. *Bofu*
16. Baby Cucumbers with Flowers
    (*Hana-tsuki-kyuri*)

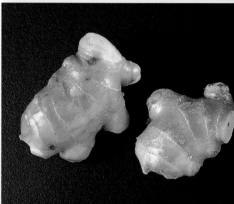

Processed Foods and Dried Foods

1. *Nori* Seaweed
2. *Kampyo* (Dried Gourd)
3. Agar-agar (*Kanten*)
4. *Wakame* Seaweed

5. *Konnyaku* (Devil's Tongue)
6. *Shiratamako*
7. *Aburage* (Tofu Puff)
8. *Kamaboko* (Fish Cakes)

9. *Udon* Noodles
10. *Yuba*
11. *Fu* (Wheat Gluten)
12. Adzuki Beans

The Basic Seasonings

Aside from sugar and salt, most basic seasonings in Japanese food are unique to Japanese cuisine. Luckily, however, such seasonings as shoyu, miso, and saké are now widely available outside of Japan, too. Although these seasonings are easy to use, knowing a little about each can help you to use them wisely.

Shoyu

Soy beans, wheat flour, *koji* (rice cultured with aspergillus mold), salt and water are fermented together to produce this widely used seasoning. Whether for dipping sashimi, basting kebabs, simmering fish or dressing salads, shoyu plays a major role in Japanese cuisine. Available in both light and dark varieties, shoyu has a smoother, milder flavor than Chinese soy sauce.

Dark Shoyu
(Koikuchi-shoyu)
This shoyu is the more common of the two kinds. If a recipe does not specify which kind of shoyu is needed, you can assume it means dark shoyu. It goes well with meat, fish, vegetables and tofu and tones down the raw smell of meat or fish. It gives such dishes as Sukiyaki and Chicken and Leek Kebabs their mouth-watering smells and rich flavors.

Light Shoyu
(Usukuchi-shoyu)
Lighter in color but with a slightly higher salt content, this shoyu does not color foods as much as regular shoyu. It is therefore preferred for dishes in which the natural colors of the foods are important, such as clear soups or simmered vegetables.

Miso
This pungent paste is made from steamed soy beans mixed with rice, wheat or bean *koji* (agents that turn starch into sugar) and salt, then fermented and aged. Like cheese in the West, miso boasts a wide range of regional variations in color, flavor, smell and texture. The most common type of miso is made from rice, and the most widely available types are red miso (actually dark brown, with widely different tastes and saltiness), and sweet white miso (a light brown paste containing less salt than other varieties.)

Aside from soup, miso is also used as a seasoning for salads, simmered and broiled dishes. It also helps to tone down the strong smells of poultry and game. Always add *miso* at the last minute when making soup to retain its smell and flavor.

When choosing miso, look for one with both a rich smell and a glossy appearance. Store in an airtight container in the refrigerator.

Japanese Rice Vinegars
(Kome-zu)
Unlike many Western varieties, Japanese vinegars are made from grains. Rice alone is used to make rice vinegar, which is known for its mildness and is commonly used for Sushi Rice and for salad dressings. Chemically reacted vinegars are also available but lack the flavor of distilled vinegars.

An alternative to vinegar which is equally refreshing is the juice of sharp citrus fruit such as *daidai, yuzu, kaposu* or *sudachi.*

Both vinegars and citrus juices stimulate the appetite and help overcome fatigue. They are also a

natural preservative and help to keep foods tasting fresh. Lastly, when sprinkled over fish, they have the effect of firming up the flesh, softening the bones, and countering fishy smells and oiliness.

Mirin
Mirin is a sweet cooking alcohol made from steamed glutinous rice (*mochi*) and *koji* mixed together with *shochu* (distilled rice, sweet potato and barley liquor). Matured for two months, it has a sweetness with a deeper, more rounded flavor than that of sugar. Mirin adds a glossy finish for such dishes as Teriyaki and Chicken and Leek Kebabs.

Saké
Also known as *nihonshu* or *seishu*, Japanese rice wine is brewed from rice, *koji* and water. It has been enjoyed as a beverage for centuries, but also plays a vital role in Japanese cooking. Aside from its rich flavor, saké tenderizes foods and tones down raw tastes or smells. Even a little saké makes a big difference to the flavor of a dish. Its alcoholic content means that it also acts as a food preservative: add some saké to a dish and it will last for several days.

Dressings, Sauces, Stocks and Soups

The most popular and widely used Japanese sauces and dressings are created from just a few basic ingredients. Below are some that are featured in recipes throughout this book.

All are low in calories and simple to make. Only one recipe contains oil, and none will curdle or go lumpy. Feel free to experiment with the ingredients or use these recipes with vegetables, meat and fish besides those suggested here.

Shoyu Dressing
Good for lightly boiled vegetables such as spinach, komatsu-na *or Chinese cabbage.*

1½ tablespoons light shoyu
¾ cup dashi stock

Sesame Dressing
For green beans, broccoli or other green vegetable salads.

4 tablespoons toasted sesame seeds
   (black or white)
1 tablespoon saké
1 tablespoon sugar
½ tablespoon shoyu
Dash of salt

Grind the sesame seeds to a paste and mix together with the other ingredients.

Mustard Dressing
For chilled vegetables, fish or chicken salads.

3 tablespoons Japanese rice vinegar
3 tablespoons light shoyu
1 tablespoon sugar
Dash of salt
2 tablespoons dashi stock
½ tablespoon mustard paste

Ginger Dressing
Use like Mustard Dressing.

2 tablespoons Japanese rice vinegar
2 tablespoons light shoyu
2 tablespoons dashi
1–2 teaspoons ginger juice
½–1 tablespoon sugar (optional)

Neri-Miso Topping : Miso Spread
Instead of eggplant (see page 122), try this topping with pan-fried tofu, daikon or turnip boiled until soft. If using red miso, double the amount of sugar used.

⅓ cup white miso
1 tablespoon sugar
⅓ cup mirin

Mix and stir over a low heat until thick.

Mustard and Miso Dressing
For boiled vegetables, shellfish or squid.

Add ⅔ tablespoon mustard paste and 1½ tablespoons Japanese rice vinegar to the ingredients for *Neri*-Miso Topping.

Chicken Kebab Sauce

½ cup mirin
¼ cup shoyu
2 tablespoons sugar

Bring the ingredients to a boil and cook for 4–5 minutes over medium heat.

Teriyaki Sauce
For fish fillets or chicken.

¼ cup saké
1 tablespoon sugar
½ cup mirin
½ cup shoyu

Tempura Sauce
Dipping sauce for Tempura.

¼ oz. (10 g) bonito flakes
1 cup water
¼ cup mirin
¼ cup light shoyu

Mix and bring to a boil. Strain immediately.

Simmering Stock for Fish

This stock is suitable for any kind of fish, but if using strong-smelling fish such as sardines or mackerel, increase the saké to ½ cup.

1 cup dashi stock or water
2 tablespoons saké
3½ tablespoons sugar
3½ tablespoons mirin
4 tablespoons shoyu

Mix and bring to a boil. Place the fish in the pot and simmer until cooked.

Clear Soup I

Sumashi-jiru

3½ cups dashi stock
1⅓ teaspoons salt
1 teaspoon light shoyu
1 teaspoon saké

Clear Soup II

Ushio-jiru
Good with clams and white fish.

3½ cups *kombu* dashi
1 rounded teaspoon salt
2 teaspoons saké

Miso Soup

Miso-shiru

3½ cups dashi stock
2½ oz. (70–80 g) miso

Stock for Seafood Stew

Yosenabe no ni-jiru

8 cups dashi stock
3 tablespoons saké
3 tablespoons light shoyu
1 rounded tablespoon salt

Ponzu Sauce

Ponsu-joyu
A tangy sauce for nabe *(one-pot dishes) such as Table-Top Chicken (see page 84) and* Shabu-Shabu. *It can also be sprinkled over lightly boiled vegetables or steamed fish.*

Equal quantities of the following:
   Sudachi, daidai, lime or lemon juice
   Shoyu
   Dashi stock

Vinegar-Shoyu Sauce

Su-joyu
Use like Ponzu sauce.

Equal quantities of the following:
   Japanese rice vinegar
   Light shoyu
   Dashi stock

Sesame Sauce

Goma-dare
Use like Ponzu Sauce.

4 tablespoons *atari-goma* sesame
   paste (or tahini)*
3½ tablespoons sugar
2 tablespoons miso
2 tablespoons shoyu
2 tablespoons saké
6 tablespoons Japanese rice vinegar
1 tablespoon sesame oil
Dash of *shichimi-togarashi*

* If unavailable, make your own by grinding 8 tablespoons of toasted white sesame seeds into a rough paste.

Sushi Rice Seasoning

Sushi-meshi no awasezu

(For 2 cups of uncooked rice)

¼ cup Japanese rice vinegar
½ tablespoon sugar
½ tablespoon salt

Cutting Vegetables

Presentation of food is elevated to an art form in Japanese cuisine. As the cutting of vegetables plays a crucial part in this, numerous ways of doing so have developed. The cook selects the cut according to the size and appearance of the ingredient, the way it will be cooked, and how easy it will be to eat with chopsticks.

The following is a list of the basic cuts and decorative cuts that add an elegant touch to any dish.

The Basic Cuts

1. Round slices (*Wa-giri*)

2. Half-moon slices (*Hangetsu-giri*)

3. Gingko leaf slices (*Icho-giri*)
Cut quarters into slices.

4. Chunks (*Butsu-giri*)

5. Rolling slices (*Ran-giri*)
Cut once on the diagonal, then turn the vegetable 90° and cut on the same diagonal again.

6. Slant slices (*Naname-giri*)

7. Sticks (*Hyoshigi-giri*)

8. Wafer-thin rectangles (*Tanzaku-giri*)

9. Square sheets (*Shikishi-giri*)

10. Dice (*Sai no me-giri*)

11. Thin round slices (*Koguchi-giri*)

12. **Threads**
(*Sen-giri*)

13. **Minced**
(*Mijin-giri*)

14. **Shavings**
(*Sasagaki*)
Shave the vegetable with a knife as if sharpening a stick.

15. **Paper-thin sheets**
(*Katsura-muki*)
Peel thinly all the way around the vegetable.

Decorative Cuts

1. **Snake's Eye** (*Janome*)
For cucumbers
Cut a cucumber into 2" (5 cm) lengths. Remove the center using an apple corer or cutter and discard. Slice the cucumber thinly. Rings can be linked like paper chains by making a small cut in each and joining them up.

2. **Twisted Plum Blossom**
(*Nejiri-ume*)
For carrots or daikon
Cut the vegetables into ½" (1 cm) wide slices. Use a plum blossom vegetable cutter to shape each slice. Score divisions between each of the five petals with a knife. Cut a small wedge from the midpoint of each petal down to the score mark to give the blossom a three-dimensional effect.

3. **Tea Whisk** (*Chasen*)
For small eggplants
With its fine twists and balloon shape, this cut is reminiscent of the *chasen*, the small bamboo whisk used to froth up green tea at a tea ceremony. This cut also helps the flavor of the stock penetrate the eggplant. Make fine vertical scores from the base of the eggplant to the top. Cook by deep-frying or simmer-ing. Drain well. While pushing the top, twist the eggplant until it fans out and stays set.

4. **Pine Needles** (*Matsuba*)
For yuzu *peel*
Cut a rectangular piece of peel approximately ⅓" x ¾" (8 mm x 2 cm). Make a lengthwise cut down the center, stopping just before the end so that the two pieces stay together.

5. **Folded Pine Needles**
(*Ore-matsuba*)
For yuzu *peel*
Cut a piece of *yuzu* peel the same size as for Pine Needles. Make a cut starting at one third in from the bottom left corner, again stopping just before the end. Then do the same from the top right corner. Twist the garnish until the two out-side pieces cross each other to form a triangle.

Filleting Fish and Slicing Sashimi

Although filleting a large fish is not advisable for the amateur chef, fish up to the size of a sea bream can be filleted at home, provided the basics have been mastered. Before starting, however, ensure that your knife is very sharp.

Japanese filleting is quite simple. First the fish is scaled and the head removed. Then the fish is cut into fillets according to its size and shape. The names of these cuts refer to the number of pieces they make. Cutting the fish in two—one half with the backbone and one half without—is called a two-piece cut (two *mai-oroshi*). But when the backbone is cut away from the flesh, this becomes a three-piece cut (three *mai-oroshi*); two fillets and the backbone. Finally, check any fillets before using, as they may still contain fine bones.

Two- and Three-Piece Cutting

This type of cut is suitable for fish with narrow but thick fillets, such as mackerel or sea bass.

1. Lay the fish on its side on a cutting board, steadying it with one hand. Insert the knife underneath the pectoral finand cut towards the head until you reach the backbone. Turn the fish over and repeat. Sever the backbone and remove the head, pulling the innards out at the same time.   **(1–3)**

2. Cut open the belly down to the tail, keeping the blade of the knife flat and just above the bones. Clean out the visceral cavity well with a damp cloth.   **(4)**

3. Cut down the length of the back, again keeping the blade just above the bones. When you reach the tail,

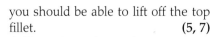

you should be able to lift off the top fillet.   **(5, 7)**

4. To make a three-piece cut, turn the lower fillet over so the backbone faces down. Cut down towards the tail between the flesh and the bones. Lift off the second fillet.   **(6, 8)**

Five-Piece Cutting

This cut is used when preparing broad but flat fish like sea bream for sashimi. It is also used for fish with delicate flesh, such as bonito, and for any flatfish.

For this cut, the two fillets from three-piece cut are cut lengthwise in half. The fillets of fragile and flat fish are cut on either side of the backbone first, then lifted off the bone separately.

1. Lay the fish on one side. Remove the scales by scraping from the tail up towards the head. Insert the knife beneath the gill cover and sever the bone below the jaw. Cut from beneath the pectoral fin towards the head until you reach the backbone. Turn the fish over and repeat. Cut off the head.   **(1–3)**
2. Slice open the belly, remove the innards and wipe out the cavity with a damp cloth. With the knife flat and just above the bones, cut towards the tail, freeing the flesh of the belly from the bones. Initially cut only as far as the backbone. Then, lifting up the flesh on this side, slice over the backbone and continue cutting away the flesh from the back.   **(4–5)**
3. Turn the other half of the fish over, so the backbone faces down. To free the flesh before removing it, first make a cut in from both the belly and the back to the backbone. Then, working towards the tail, cut the flesh away from the back to the backbone. Lifting the back up, cut away the flesh from the belly.   **(6)**
4. Cut the two fillets lengthwise in half. If preparing sashimi, remove the skin. To do so, lay the fish skin side down. Insert the knife between the skin and the flesh at the tail end. Move it slowly up the fish as you pull the skin off with your hand. **(7–8)**

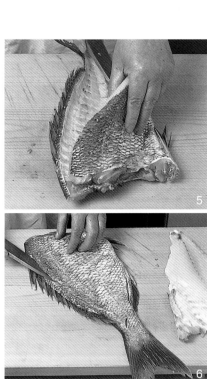

Sashimi Cuts

Flat Cuts
(Hira-zukuri)
These ⅜" (1 cm) thick slabs are the most conventional cut for sashimi. A block of tuna fillet gives regular rectangular slices, but flat cuts from fish cut into five-piece cut taper at the end.

As sashimi is extremely delicate, even the angle of the knife is important. Insert the heel of the knife into the closest edge of the fish. As you lower the knife, draw it swiftly towards you. Cut slices about ⅜" (1 cm) wide.

Square Cuts
(Kaku-zukuri)
These ¾" (2 cm) squares are a suitable cut for fish with a thick, soft flesh, such as tuna and bonito.

Slant Slices
(Sogi-zukuri)
This kind of thin slicing is suitable for fish such as sea bream, sole, flounder and sea bass. It is not angular like the other cuts, but more closely follows the shape of the fish fillet.

Lay the fish skin side upwards. Holding the knife at a sharp angle, place the heel on the closest edge of the fish. As you lower the knife, draw it towards you. Cut slices ⅛"–⅜" (2 mm–1 cm) wide.

Another cut which is the same shape but only paper-thin is *usu-zukuri*. Sashimi cut this way is so thin that any design on the plate below can be seen through it.

Flat Cuts
(Hira-zukuri)

Square Cuts
(Kaku-zukuri)

Slant Slices
(Sogi-zukuri)

Making Dashi Stock

Dashi is a fundamental ingredient of Japanese soups and simmered dishes. It is used more frequently than Western stocks and bouillons, appearing in dressings and sauces where Western cuisine might use oil instead.

The more dashi required by the recipe, the more important the quality of the dashi becomes. While instant dashi is fine for use in small quantities, try to resist the temptation of using it when making a clear soup, for example.

Kombu and Bonito Dashi
This is the classic method for making dashi. In contrast to the slow simmering needed to make Western stocks, it is important to extract the flavors for dashi swiftly. If the *kombu* and bonito flakes are boiled for too long, the dashi becomes cloudy and strong-smelling.

4" (10 cm) square sheet thick *kombu*
1 oz. (30 g) bonito flakes
6 cups water

1. Wipe the *kombu* lightly to remove dust or dirt. Leave the white powdery coating, as this is contains much of the flavor of *kombu*. **(1–2)**
2. Place the water and *kombu* in a pan and bring to the boil over a medium heat. Remove the *kombu* just before the mixture reaches boiling point. **(3)**
3. Drop the bonito flakes into the center of the bubbling stock. Turn down the heat after 3–4 seconds. Skim off any scum carefully and strain the stock immediately to remove the bonito flakes. **(4–7)**

* Using both *kombu* and bonito flakes produces the most flavorful stock, as the two ingredients have a complementary effect on each other. Bonito flakes can be used alone, however, if *kombu* is unavailable. Add the bonito flakes to boiling water. Boil briefly and strain.

Kombu Stock

Kombu produces a light refreshing stock merely by being soaked in cold water for a few hours. This stock is used in dishes where the natural flavors of the ingredients are savored, such as Clear Clam Soup (see page 56). It is also used in Zen-style vegetarian cooking.

4" x 8" (10 cm x 20 cm) sheet *kombu*
4 cups water

1. Wipe the *kombu* only lightly to remove any dust or dirt.
2. Leave it to soak in the water. In winter it will take about 4 hours for the flavor to be released; in summer, about two. On very hot days, it is a good idea to refrigerate the *kombu* while it soaks. Remove the *kombu* before using the stock.　　　　**(8)**

Commercial Dashi Stocks

Instant stocks come in granulated and liquid forms and need only to be mixed with hot water. While instant stock can never match the flavor of homemade stock, it is convenient when you do not have the ingredients for real dashi or only need a small quantity. As instant dashi is highly concentrated, take care not to add too much.

Kitchen Equipment

Although Western frying pans jostle with Chinese steamers in the average Japanese kitchen today, you will also find several uniquely Japanese utensils. Substitutes are easily found for some, but others, such as an omelet pan or a earthenware casserole, may be a practical investment if you plan to use them often.

Bamboo Drainer
Bonzaru
A flat woven bamboo container which dips slightly in the center. Used for rinsing or draining cooked ingredients, it is also handy for salting and draining fish slices.   **(1)**

Bamboo Mat
Makisu
Used to roll Japanese omelets or sushi rolls, this pliable mat consists of thin strips of bamboo woven with thread into a rectangle. It is also used for rolling and squeezing out excess water in boiled vegetables.
Substitute: Use a laminated place mat, a piece of bamboo blind or a strong kitchen towel.   **(3)**

Cooking Chopsticks
Saibashi
Used for cooking and serving, these chopsticks are longer than eating chopsticks. Made from bamboo, they do not burn easily, nor do they allow food to slip out of their grasp. **(5)**

Cutters
Nukigata
Small cutters are used to shape vegetable garnishes. Larger ones are used for rice and have lids with handles to make pushing out the cut rice easier.   **(7)**

Drop Lid
Otoshi-buta
Because Japanese aluminum saucepans do not come with their own lids, drop lids are used when simmering foods. They are so named because they are slightly smaller than the pan and drop directly onto the food. Simmering this way ensures more even cooking, while the slight gap between the lid and the edge of the pan means that overboiling is rare.   **(9)**
Substitute: Use aluminum foil or parchment paper to cover the food as tightly as possible.

Earthenware Casserole
Do-nabe
Used for the wide range of one pot dishes (*nabe*) that are cooked at the table. It spreads the heat gently and evenly, so that even after being removed from the heat dishes stay warm for a long time. There are myriad designs and sizes of earthenware casseroles, to suit the wide range of Japanese *nabe* dishes.   **(2)**
Substitute: An electric skillet or fondue pot.

Grater
Oroshiki
Aside from the universal flat grater, there is another peculiarly Japanese kind: a grater sitting over its own shallow dish to collect the grated vegetable. Use the fine teeth for ginger or *wasabi* and the larger teeth for *daikon*.   **(4)**

Japanese Omelet Pan
Tamago-yaki-nabe
A square or rectangular pan used for cooking and rolling Japanese omelets. Traditionally made of copper, many are nowadays made of Teflon.
Substitute: Use a regular frying pan and trim the omelet after rolling.

Japanese Pestle and Mortar
Suri-bachi and *Surikogi*
Used for grinding such ingredients as sesame seeds or for blending ingredients. The base of the mortar is narrower than the top and the inside has fine vertical ridges, making it easier to grind the food. The pestle is made of wood. Both come in a variety of sizes.   **(6)**
Substitute: A food-processor.

Knives
Hocho
Good knives are a must for any kitchen. Although there are many kinds of knives, the most commonly used Japanese knife is *wa-bocho* (*hocho*). It has a tapered blade and is used for cutting vegetables (*nakiri-bocho*), meat and fish.

Another knife indispensable to the Japanese cook is the *deba-bocho*, a heavy carving knife used to fillet fish and cut through meat—even bones.

Lastly, there is the wide cleaver with a rectangular blade called a *saikirihocho*. The shape of its blade makes for easy shredding or chopping of vegetables.   **(8)**

Rice Paddle
Kijakushi or *shamoji*
Whether for mixing ingredients or serving rice and cooked dishes, a paddle is a versatile tool to have around the kitchen. It is gentler to rice than a metal spoon.   **(5)**
Substitute: A wooden spoon or a plastic spatula.

Saucepan, Aluminum

Katate-nabe or *yukihira*

Often used for soups, simmered dishes and for marinating, this pan's wooden handle and spout make it easy to use. When buying, look for as heavy a pan as possible. Also, having a set of small, medium and large pans comes in very handy.   **(9)**
Substitute: A regular saucepan.

Sukiyaki pan

Sukiyaki-nabe

A flat-based cast-iron pan used only for Sukiyaki.
Substitute: A heavy-based casserole dish.

Sushi Rice Pail

Handai, hangiri or *sushi-oke*

A shallow wooden container for mixing cooked rice with vinegar, sugar and salt for sushi. Because the wood is unvarnished, it absorbs any excess moisture and leaves the finished rice perfect.   **(10)**
Substitute: Any shallow dish.

Japanese Tableware

The choice of tableware plays a significant role in the all-important presentation of Japanese food. Japanese tableware therefore comes in a much wider variety of shapes, sizes, colors and materials than that of the West. Bowls and plates may be made of earthenware, china, lacquerware or bamboo, for example. They may be circular, triangular, hexagonal or even flower-shaped. While a Western household may pride itself on having a matching dinner service, a Japanese cook would generally choose individual pieces of tableware which best match the season and each dish to be served.

Bowls

Deep bowls are used for simmered foods, salads, dishes with sauces or dishes which must be kept warm. Large bowls are used as serving dishes; medium-sized ones, for a serving of a simmered dish, salad or pickle; and small ones are used when helping oneself from a dish in the center of the table. These small bowls are also used for dipping sauces. Bowls may be made of fairly thick earthenware, delicate and almost translucent china or lacquerware. Glass bowls are used for serving chilled dishes.

Rice Bowls and *Domburi* Bowls

A rice bowl holds a single serving of rice. It is an easy shape both to hold and to eat from when using chopsticks. Everyday rice bowls do not have a lid, but those used for visitors sometimes do. Larger bowls are for serving *domburi* (meat, Tempura or egg on a bed of rice) or noodles.

Plates

Broiled or deep-fried dishes and simmered fish are generally served on plates. These may be flat or deep and come in a variety of shapes and colors. Round, square and rectangular plates are fairly common, but diamond-shaped plates, plates with handles and even leaf-shaped plates can also be found. Like Japanese bowls, large plates are used as serving dishes; medium ones, for a single serving; and small plates are for helping oneself from a serving dish. Small plates are also used for shoyu when serving sashimi.

Lacquerware and Bamboo

Lacquered wooden bowls are primarily used for soups. Light and easy to hold, they also prevent soup from cooling down too quickly. The smooth lacquer and the natural wood makes holding and drinking from these lacquered wooden bowls very pleasurable.

Trays used either for carrying dishes to the table or for a place setting may also be made of lacquerware.

Bamboo is another natural material used in Japanese tableware. The shape of a dish may follow the natural contours of the bamboo, while baskets are woven from split bamboo. These dishes may be used for Tempura and other deep-fried foods, rice rolls, sushi or any dishes without juices or sauces.

Saké Flasks and Cups

The small bottle-shaped container for pouring saké is called a *tokkuri*, while the metal or ceramic teapot-shaped container with a handle and a spout is called a *kannabe*. The tiny cups for drinking saké are referred to as *sakazuki*. They come in a variety of shapes and can be made of earthenware, lacquerware or glass.

Teacups and Teapots

A teapot for Japanese green tea is called a *kyusu*, and can be made of earthenware, china or metal. Teacups are made either of earthenware or china, and are called *chawan*.

Chopsticks

In addition to eating chopsticks, there are also slightly longer serving chopsticks. Chopsticks may be made of a wood like Japanese cedar or willow, or of bamboo or lacquerware.

Eating chopsticks are laid on a chopstick rest to prevent soiling the table. These rests come in a variety of designs, including ones for seasonal use.

Other tableware items which might appear at mealtimes are the various bottles, dishes, pots and bowls for such condiments as shoyu, *shichimi-togarashi* and mustard. These vary according to the food being served.

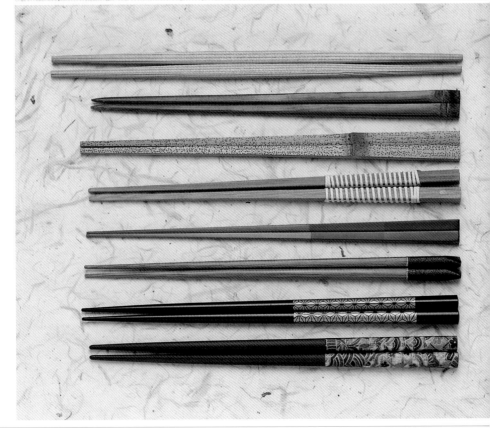

I
SEASONAL MENUS

A Picnic Lunch for Spring
A Refreshing Summer Buffet
A Harvesttime Dinner
A Winter Feast

A Picnic Lunch for Spring

Top Box:
Red and white *kamaboko*,
Shrimp, Cucumber and *Wakame* in Ginger
Dressing, see page 117,
Pickled white radish,
Gourd-Shaped Eggs, see page 86

Middle Box:
Green Fried Chicken, see page 81,
Salmon Rolls, see page 44

Bottom Box:
Molded rice
Clear Clam Soup,
see page 56

A Refreshing Summer Buffet

Avocado with Mustard-Shoyu
Dressing, see page 51,
Beef Tataki, see page 48,
Summer Vegetables *Takiawase*,
see page 124,
Savory Steamed Custard (Chilled),
see page 89,
Savory Rice Balls, see page 132
and
Fruit Salad with Silky Rice Drops,
see page 144

A Harvest-time Dinner

Shoyu-Steeped Spinach, see page 118,
Clear Chicken and mushroom
Soup, see page 54,
Harvest Rice, see page 129,
Shoyu-Broiled Butterfish, see page 45,
Braised Chicken Balls and Turnips,
see page 82
and
Sweet Potato Candy,
see page 146

A Winter Feast

II
FROM
APPETIZERS
TO
DESSERTS

Assorted Appetizers
Zensai no moriawase

These delicate dishes combine ingredients from both land and sea: fish, seaweeds, nuts, fruits and vegetables. They should be attractively presented, as appearance is fundamental to Japanese cuisine.

Roast Duck, Japanese Style
Kamo no wafu rosuto

1 *aigamo* duck or ordinary duck, about 11–14 oz. (300–400 g)
½ teaspoon vegetable oil
SEASONINGS:
  3 cups water
  ½ cup saké
  1 cup shoyu
  Dash of salt
Mustard to serve

1. Remove excess skin and fat from the duck and pat into shape. Prick the skin all over with a fork. (1–2)
2. Heat the oil in a frying pan. Add the duck with the skin side down. Cook over medium heat for 5–6 minutes. Once the skin has browned and fat has begun to ooze out, turn over. Continue to cook for about 1 minute. (3)
3. Place duck in a colander. Pour boiling water over both sides of the duck to get rid of fat. (4)
4. Put the seasonings and the duck in a small pan and bring to a boil over medium heat. Lower the heat and continue to cook for 6–7 minutes, occasionally skimming the scum off the surface. (5)
5. Remove the duck from the broth and leave to cool. Once cool, return the duck to the broth. Marinade in broth overnight. (6)
6. Cut the duck into ⅛" (3 mm) slices and arrange on a serving plate. Serve with mustard on the side.

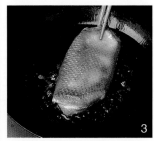

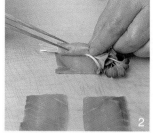

Salmon Flowers with Salmon Rolls
Smoku samon ni-shu

8 slices smoked salmon, approx. 5 oz. (150 g)
Finely sifted egg yolk, see page 46
2 oz. (50 g) *daikon* sprouts
Mi-zansho no tsukudani or capers

For the salmon rolls:
1. Run the *daikon* sprouts under cold water to remove the seeds and drain. Cut off the ends. **(1)**
2. Cut four of the salmon slices into 3" (7.5 cm) slices.
3. Lay 7 or 8 *daikon* sprouts on each salmon slice and roll up tightly from one end. **(2)**
4. Garnish with *mi-zansho no tsukudani* or capers.

For the salmon flowers:
1. Cut the remaining salmon slices into 2" (5 cm) lengths. Slice each strip horizontally in half.
2. Form "flowers" by tightly rolling up 3–4 salmon strips together. **(3)**
3. Curl the upper edges of the "flowers" to resemble petals. **(4)**
4. Sprinkle egg yolk in the middle.

Crunchy Walnuts in *Kombu* Baskets
Age kurumino kombu-kago mori

10 shelled walnuts
4 *kombu* baskets*
2 cups vegetable oil for deep-frying
Dash of salt

1. Heat the oil to 300°F (150°C) and deep-fry each *kombu* basket for 5–6 seconds. Remove and and drain well.
2. Deep-fry walnuts for 10 seconds. **(1)** Remove quickly and drain. Sprinkle with salt and divide between the *kombu* baskets.

* *Kombu* baskets consist of thinly sliced *kombu* woven into the shape of a basket. They are available at specialized Japanese food stores.

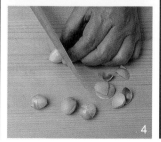

Three-Color Kebabs
Kushizashi

8 small live shrimp
  Dash of salt
3 baby cucumbers (*morokyu*),
  2½–3" (7–8 cm) long
1 tablespoon salt
8 gingko nuts, shelled
  Dash of salt
8 bamboo skewers

1. With the shrimp lying underside up, slice deeply beneath the head of each. Pull off the heads and devein.
2. Bring a large pot of water to a boil. Add salt, then the shrimp. Approximately 30 seconds after the water returns to a boil, remove the shrimp and allow to cool. Shell the shrimp but leave the tails intact. **(1)**
3. Place the baby cucumbers on a chopping board, sprinkle with salt and firmly roll them back and forth to soften them. Immerse in boiling water, then plunge immediately into cold water so they turn bright green. **(2)**
4. In a small pan, boil just enough water to cover the gingko nuts. Add a dash of salt, then the nuts. Stir with a slotted spoon. Drain and peel the thin skin off the nuts. Allow to cool in a colander. **(3–4)**
5. Remove tails from the shrimp. Cut the cucumbers into 1" (2 cm) lengths. Thread a piece of cucumber, a shrimp and a gingko nut onto each bamboo skewer.

Salmon Roe in Citrus Cups
Ikura no sudachi-zume

4 rounded tablespoons salted salmon
  roe (*ikura*)*
½ tablespoon saké
4 *sudachi* or limes
GARNISH:
  Bofu or other green leaves

1. Slice off the top of each *sudachi* to form a lid. Thinly slice off the bottom of

each fruit to flatten.
2. Carefully cut away the inside flesh of each *sudachi* and scoop out with a small spoon. **(1–2)**
3. Sprinkle the saké over the salmon roe and heap it into the *sudachi* "cups." Garnish with *bofu* or other small green leaves. Rest the *sudachi* lids against the cups.

* Red caviar can be substituted for salted salmon roe.

Shoyu-Broiled Butterfish
Managatsuo no shoyu-yaki

2 *managatsuo* (butterfish) fillets
  (approx. 11 oz., 300–350 g)
MARINADE AND GLAZE:
  3 tablespoons saké
  3 tablespoons mirin
  7 tablespoons shoyu
  ½ *yuzu* or lime, sliced
GARNISH:
  4 pickled ginger shoots (*sudori-shoga*)*

1. Cut the *managatsuo* fillets in half lengthwise. Then, tilting the knife slightly, cut crosswise into 4 or 5 small slices. **(1)**
2. Mix together the ingredients for the marinade in a shallow dish. Add the *yuzu* slices, then the fish and cover. Marinate for an hour, turning the fish several times to ensure even coverage. **(2)**
3. Preheat the oven to 480°F (250°C). Place a rack on a baking tray. Lay the *managatsuo* slices on the rack and cook for 7–8 minutes. **(3)**
4. Brush both sides of the fish well with marinade and cook for a further 3–4 minutes to glaze. Arrange on a plate and garnish with pickled ginger shoots. **(4)**

*Sudori-shoga are young ginger shoots preserved or soaked in sweet vinegar.

Assorted Sashimi
Sashimi no moriawase

Raw fish is a unique feature of Japanese cuisine. To enjoy sashimi at its best, choose fresh seasonal fish.

11 oz. (300 g) tuna fillet, 1" x 2½"
   (2.5 cm x 6 cm)
11 oz. (300 g) sea bream, skinned and
   cut into a five-piece cut, see page 21
3½ oz. (100 g) shelled sea urchin
GARNISHES:
   1 boiled egg for *kimisoboro*
   Daikon
   Seaweed (*akaito-nori, suizenji-nori,* etc.)
   1 lime
   Shiso, bofu, shiso shoots, *shiso* seed
      pods, *beni-tade, me-negi,* etc.
Wasabi and mustard to serve

1. Cut ⅔ of the tuna into slices just over ½" (1 cm) wide for flat-cut sashimi (*hira-zukuri*). Cut the remainder into squares of approximately 1" x 1" (2 cm x 2 cm) for square-cut sashimi (*kaku-zukuri*). **(1–2)**
2. Cut ⅔ of the sea bream into flat cuts, like the tuna. Slice the rest at a slant for slant-cut sashimi (*sogi-zukuri*). **(3)**
3. Press the yolk of the boiled egg through a small sieve. **(4)**
4. Using a sharp knife, peel round and round the *daikon* radish to form long thin sheets (*katsura-muki,* see page 19). Roll these sheets up and slice into long, fine threads. Soak in cold water. **(5–6)**
5. Heap the *akaito-nori* seaweed and drained *daikon* threads at the back of the serving dish. Stand a green *shiso* leaf upright against the *daikon* and arrange the flat-cut and square-cut tuna in front of the *shiso* leaf.
6. Arrange the flat-cut sea bream in front of the tuna. Dip the slant-cut sea bream in the egg yolk and place in mounds at the front and back of the dish.
7. Cut the lime in half. Scoop out the flesh from one half and fill with the sea urchin. Place it to the left.

8. Arrange such garnishes as *me-negi,* small green sprouting *shiso, bofu* and young *shiso* spikes on and around the sashimi and add dabs of *wasabi* and mustard.
9. Serve each guest with a small dish of shoyu. Guests can then add *wasabi* and mustard to the shoyu according to taste. (*Wasabi* goes well with tuna, seabream and sea urchin, while mustard adds a tang to tuna.) Dip the sashimi in the shoyu before eating.

Garnishes for Sashimi
Sashimi no tsuma
There are three kinds of vegetables and seaweed in a sashimi assortment: *ken, tsuma,* and *karami.* These garnishes are not only for decoration; they also serve to bring out the flavor of the fish and to boost the nutritional content of the dish.

Ken is the bed of finely shredded vegetables on which the sashimi is arranged. Usually, the *ken* is made from *daikon* radish, but it may be replaced by cucumber, carrot or *udo.* The *ken* sets off the arrangement visually, as well as balancing the flavors. It is also reputed to aid digestion.

Tsuma may include green *shiso* leaves, small green sprouting *shiso, beni-tade,* young *shiso* spikes, *bofu, me-negi* and various seaweeds. They add color and distinctive flavors to a sashimi arrangement. (The word "*tsuma*" is also used to refer to sashimi garnishes in general.)

Wasabi is the most common *karami.* However, for strong-smelling fish and squid, mustard or fresh root ginger may be used instead. *Karami* adds a piquancy to sashimi while helping to keep the fish tasting fresh.

Beef Tataki
Gyuniku no tataki

Pan-fried quickly so that only the outside is browned while the inside remains rare, this beef is sliced wafer-thin and served like sashimi.

11 oz. (300 g) beef, boneless round,
  1″ x 2½″ (3 cm x 6 cm)
¼ teaspoon salt
Dash of pepper
½ tablespoon vegetable oil
1 tablespoon saké
2 tablespoons shoyu
6 *asatsuki* or green onions
1–2 cloves garlic
1″ (2.5 cm) slice of fresh ginger root
½ cup grated daikon with chilli
  peppers (*momiji-oroshi*), see page 154

1. Sprinkle the beef with salt and pepper and rub in well.   **(1)**
2. Heat the frying pan over low heat. Add the oil. Swirl until the surface of the pan is evenly coated. Turn the heat up to medium and add the beef. Shaking the pan gently, fry the meat quickly until both sides are evenly browned. Remove from heat.   **(2–3)**
3. Sprinkle the saké and shoyu over the meat and cover as tightly as possible with a bowl just big enough to cover the meat. Cook over low heat for 6–7 minutes, then remove the meat.   **(4–6)**
4. Slightly reduce the gravy in the frying pan and pour over the meat. Leave to cool.   **(7–8)**
5. Slice off 2½″ (6 cm) lengths from the tips of the *asatsuki* and set aside. Finely mince the rest.
6. Cut 4–5 thin slices of garlic and grate the rest. Peel the ginger and grate.
7. Slice the cooled meat as thinly as possible.   **(9)**
8. Fold each slice in half and arrange in a circle on a large plate, working from the center outwards. Place a little of the minced *asatsuki*, garlic and ginger on each slice. Arrange the *momiji-oroshi* in

a mound in the center and decorate with the garlic slices and *asatsuki* tips set aside earlier.

9. At the table, pour the sauce over the meat. Allow guests to serve themselves, rolling up the garnishes in a slice of beef.

Clams and *Wakegi* in Miso Dressing

Hamaguri to wakegi no nuta

The flavors of clams and *wakegi* marry very well. Combined with a miso and mustard dressing, this makes an ideal dish for a spring day.

12 shucked clams
  Dash of salt
  1 tablespoon saké
  ½ tablespoon rice vinegar
11 oz. (300 g) *wakegi* or green onions
  Dash of salt
WHITE MISO DRESSING:
  2½ oz. (70 g) white miso
  1 tablespoon sugar
  ¼ cup mirin
  1 tablespoon mustard
  1½ tablespoons rice vinegar
GARNISH:
  8–12 sprigs *kinome*

1. To drain the clams, stick a cooking chopstick into the siphon of each. Wash clams by swirling the chopsticks in 3 cups of salted water.   **(1)**

2. Put the clams in a pan, pour over saké, and boil rapidly for about 20 seconds. When clams puff up, transfer to a colander. Sprinkle with vinegar and allow to cool.   **(2)**

3. Bring plenty of water to a boil and add salt. Gradually immerse the *wakegi*, starting with the white ends, then turn them over and after 2 seconds, remove and drain in a colander.   **(3)**

4. Lay the *wakegi* on a chopping board. Squeeze out any stickiness from the green parts by pressing with a knife toward the ends. Cut into 1"(3 cm) lengths.

5. Mix together the miso, sugar and mirin.

6. Cook over low heat, stirring with a wooden spoon, until the mixture becomes the consistency of miso. Transfer to a bowl and allow to cool. ➤

Avocado with Mustard-Shoyu Dressing

Abokado no karashi-joyu-ae

Ripe avocados are given a Japanese flavor in this simple but delicious salad.

2 avocados
MUSTARD-SHOYU DRESSING:
  ½ tablespoon mustard
  1½ tablespoons shoyu
  ½ tablespoon saké
GARNISH:
  2–3 tablespoons *beni-tade*

➤ **7.** Add the mustard and vinegar to the dressing and blend well.
8. Just before serving, mix the clams and *wakegi* with the dressing. Heap servings in bowls and garnish with *kinome*.

1. Cut the avocados lengthwise in half. Pull apart and remove the stones. Peel the avocados and cut the flesh into 1" (3 cm) cubes.   **(1–3)**
2. Mix the dressing in a bowl. Add the avocado and mix roughly. Arrange in bowls and sprinkle with *beni-tade.*

Clear Egg and *Kamaboko* Soup

Shime-tamago to kamaboko no sumashi-jiru

A light and colorful soup of egg, red and white *kamaboko* and fresh spring vegetables.

3 eggs
8 pieces *kamaboko,* each measuring
  ¼" x 4" (6 mm x 10 cm)
A few drops of red food coloring
4 fresh *shiitake* mushrooms
12 stalks *mitsuba*
CLEAR SOUP:
  3½ cups dashi
  1⅓ teaspoons salt
  1 teaspoon light shoyu
  1 teaspoon saké
GARNISH:
  4 sprigs *kinome*

1. Beat the eggs with a little salt.
2. Bring a large pot of water to a boil. Line a colander with a clean dishcloth. Once the water comes to a boil, gently pour the egg over the surface of the water. When it floats back to the surface, remove from heat. Pour through the cloth-lined colander, so that the drained egg remains on the cloth. **(1–2)**
3. Roll up the cloth. Twist both ends of the cloth and wrap the roll in a bamboo mat to shape it. Leave until cool to allow the egg to set. **(3–5)**
4. Pour 2 cups of water into a small dish and add the red food coloring. Soak 4 of the pieces of *kamaboko* until they turn red. Rinse and pat dry. Tie each piece of red *kamaboko* with a white piece in a decorative knot. **(6–8)**
5. Wipe the caps of the *shiitake* mushrooms and twist off the stems. Blanch in boiling water. **(9)**
6. Cut the *mitsuba* into 2½" (6 cm) lengths. Trim the ends of the egg roll and cut into 4 equal slices.
7. Bring the dashi to a boil. Add the *shiitake* mushrooms and the remaining ingredients for the soup. Gently add the

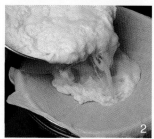

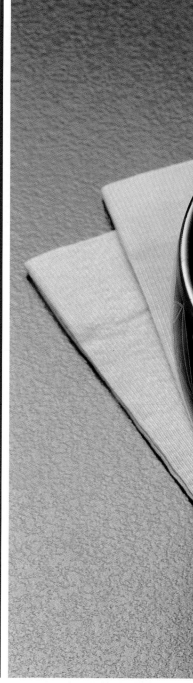

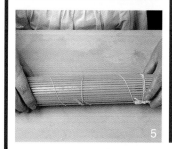

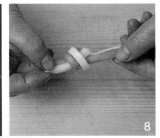

egg and *kamaboko* knots and heat through.

8. Divide the egg and *kamaboko* knots between the four bowls. Place the *shiitake* mushrooms and *mitsuba* in front. Ladle over the soup until the bowls are about ¾ full. Garnish each with a sprig of *kinome*.

Clear Chicken and Mushroom Soup

Tori sasami to shimeji no sumashi-jiru

The mild flavor and low fat content of chicken make this a smooth and delicate soup. Dusted in *katakuriko* (potato starch) before cooking, the chicken remains tender and moist.

7 oz. (200 g) chicken breast
  1 teaspoon light shoyu
  2 teaspoons saké
Katakuriko or cornstarch for coating
3½ oz. (100 g) *shimeji* mushrooms
2 oz. (60 g) *daikon* sprouts
3 cups dashi stock
SEASONINGS:
  1 teaspoon salt
  1 teaspoon light shoyu
GARNISH:
  4 strips *yuzu* peel, each about
    ⅓" x ¾" (8 mm x 2 cm)

1. Skin and bone the chicken. Cut it into bite-size pieces, sprinkle with the shoyu, saké and salt and let stand for about 5 minutes. **(1)**
2. Pat each piece of chicken all over with a piece of folded gauze containing *katakuriko*. Drop the chicken pieces in a pot of boiling water and cook over low heat until they float to the surface. Scoop them out, immerse in cold water and drain. **(2–3)**
3. Remove the base from the *shimeji* mushrooms and break the mushrooms into small clumps.
4. Rinse the *daikon* sprouts under running water and cut off the bottom. Divide into four, using one sprout to tie up each bunch. **(4–5)**
5. Cut each *yuzu* strip lengthwise to about ⅛" (3 mm) from the end. This garnish is called "pine needle *yuzu*" (*matsuba yuzu*).
6. Bring the dashi stock to a boil and add the *shimeji* mushrooms. When the dashi boils again, season with the salt

and light shoyu. Add the chicken, then the *daikon* sprouts and remove from heat immediately. Arrange the chicken, *shimeji* mushrooms and *daikon* sprouts in bowls and pour over the soup. Garnish each serving with the pine needle *yuzu*.

Clear Soups:
The main ingredient of a clear soup is called the *wan-dane*. Both bland and strong-tasting foods—egg, tofu, chicken and fish—can serve as *wan-dane*.

The vegetables providing the splash of color in a clear soup are referred to as *wan-zuma*.

Suikuchi are seasonal garnishes. The *kinome* used in this recipe heralds springtime, fine slivers of ginger or green *shiso* refresh palates in the summer and aromatic *yuzu* is the favorite in fall and winter. Use just enough *suikuchi* to add a hint of its fragrance to the food.

Clear Clam Soup
Hamaguri no ushio-jiri

Made from *kombu* stock, this light clear soup brings out the flavor of fresh seafood beautifully.

8 live hardshell clams*
  8 cups lukewarm water
  1 tablespoon salt
1½"–2" (4–5 cm) *udo*
  Water and vinegar mixture (½ table-
    spoon vinegar to 3 cups water)
3½ cups *kombu* stock, see page 22
1 teaspoon salt
2 teaspoons saké
GARNISH:
  4 sprigs *kinome*

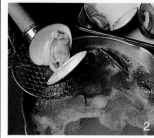

1. Soak the clams in lukewarm salted water until they expel any sand. Scrub the clams with a brush under running water. **(1)**

2. Peel the *udo* thickly and soak in the water and vinegar mixture for 5 minutes. Cut the *udo* lengthwise in half, then into thin strips. Soak again in a fresh water and vinegar mixture to remove bitterness.

3. Place the dashi and clams in a saucepan and bring to a boil. Lower the heat and skim off any scum. As soon as the clams open, remove from heat. **(2)**

4. Strain the soup through a fine sieve lined with a clean dishcloth. **(3)**

5. Return the stock to the pot. Heat and season with the salt and saké.

6. Cut the clams from their shells. Put one open shell into each soup bowl and lay a clam in each half of the shell. Place the *udo* slices in front. Ladle over the hot soup and garnish each bowl with a sprig of *kinome*. **(4)**

* Tap the shells to determine if the clams are still alive; if so, the shells should make a clear hollow sound.

Tofu and Leek Miso Soup

Tofu to negi no miso-shiru

For breakfast, lunch or dinner, a simple but nutritious miso soup still forms part of the daily diet for millions of Japanese. But it need not be boring; just add vegetables, tofu, seaweed or shellfish for variety.

½ block tofu, about 5–7 oz.
  (150–200 g)
½ leek
3½ cups dashi stock
2½ oz. (70–80 g) miso

1. Cut the tofu into ½" (1 cm) cubes and the leek into ⅛" (3 mm) slices. **(1)**
2. Heat the dashi in a saucepan. Put the miso in a sieve and force it into the soup with a pestle. Lower the heat while mixing it in for better flavor. **(2)**
3. Add the tofu. When the soup comes to a boil, add the leeks and remove from heat. Serve immediately. **(3–4)**

* Since the salt content of the four main types of miso varies greatly, always start with less than specified in the recipe. Mix, taste, then continue to add, if necessary.

Miso Soup with Cabbage and Tofu Puffs

Kyabetsu to aburage no miso-shiru

The distinctive flavor of *aburage* (tofu puff) goes well with mild-tasting vegetables such as cabbage.

7 oz. (200 g) cabbage (whole leaves)
1 sheet *aburage*
3 cups dashi stock
2½ oz. (70 g) miso

1. Cut each cabbage leaf lengthwise into four, removing the hard stalk. Pile up the leaves and cut crosswise into ¾" (2 cm) wide strips. **(1)**
2. Place the *aburage* in a colander and pour boiling water over it. Drain and cut lengthwise in half, and then crosswise into ¼" (6 mm) wide strips. **(2)**
3. Heat the dashi in a pan. Add the cabbage and cook over medium heat for 3 minutes. Add the *aburage* and cook for a further 2 minutes. **(3)**
4. Sieve the miso into the soup. Stir until dissolved. When the soup begins to boil again, remove from heat and serve immediately. **(4)**

Pork and Miso Soup
Ton-jiru or *Buta-jiru*

This nutritious and hearty soup is packed full of meat and vegetables. It is a popular family dish, especially in cold weather.

5 oz. (150 g) sliced pork shoulder or ham (approx. ⅕", 5 mm thick)
7 oz. (200 g) potatoes
2 oz. (50 g) burdock (*gobo*)
Vinegar and water mixture as needed (⅓ teaspoon vinegar to 3 cups water)
3½ oz. (100 g) *daikon*
2 oz. (60 g) carrot
⅓ block *konnyaku*
1 tablespoon vegetable oil
2 *wakegi* or green onions
4 cups dashi stock or water
3 oz. (90 g) miso
1 tablespoon saké
Shichimi-togarashi or powdered *sansho* to serve

1. Cut the pork into ½" (3 cm) wide strips. Peel the potatoes and cut lengthwise into four, then crosswise into pieces ¾" (2 cm) wide. Soak the potatoes in water for 10 minutes.
2. To clean the burdock, scrub with a brush. Cut into thin diagonal slices and leave to soak in the vinegared water. After about 5 minutes, the liquid will turn dark brown. Drain and refill with fresh mixture. Repeat 2 or 3 times to remove any bitterness.   **(1)**
3. Peel the *daikon* and cut into gingko leaf slices (*icho-giri*) approximately ¼" (5–6 mm) wide. Peel the carrot and cut into half moon slices (*hangetsu-giri*) ¼" (5–6 mm) wide.
4. Put the *konnyaku* in a saucepan with water to cover. Bring to a boil and cook for about 5 minutes. Remove and soak in cold water briefly. Tear the *konnyaku* into pieces about ½" (1 cm) wide.   **(2)**
5. Cut the *wakegi* into 1" (3 cm) lengths.   **(3)**
6. Heat the oil in a large pan. Remove from heat and rest on a damp cloth to

cool the pan slightly. Add the pork, return to the heat and stir-fry. **(4)**

7. Once the meat has changed color, add the *konnyaku* and all of the vegetables, except for the *wakegi*. Continue to stir-fry, mixing well. **(5)**

8. Pour in the dashi stock. Bring to a boil, skimming the surface occasionally, then reduce the heat. Simmer until the vegetables are tender. **(6–7)**

9. Dissolve the miso in the soup and season with the saké. Scatter the *wakegi* over the soup and remove from heat. Serve generous helpings and sprinkle with *shichimi-togarashi* or powdered *sansho* if desired. **(8)**

Salt-Broiled Salmon
Sake no shio-yaki

This dish could not be simpler: the salmon is merely sprinkled with salt and then broiled. It is therefore crucial to use the best salmon possible and to serve it immediately.

1¾ lb. (750 g) salmon fillet*
1 slightly rounded tablespoon salt
GARNISHES:
  8 *shishi-togarashi* peppers
  Pine needles or greens (optional)
SEASONINGS:
  ½ tablespoon saké
  ½ tablespoon light shoyu

1. Cut the salmon lengthways in half. Cut each half crosswise into four.   **(1)**
2. Pat the salmon dry in a colander and sprinkle with salt on both sides. Let stand for 5 minutes.   **(2)**
3. Preheat the oven to 480°F (250°C). Place the salmon on a wire rack over a baking tray and broil. When it begins to turn a golden-brown, cover with aluminum foil and broil for another 7-8 minutes.   **(3–4)**
4. Trim the stalks of the *shishi-togarashi* peppers and pierce the skin of each two or three times to prevent them from bursting during cooking. Broil directly under the broiler until cooked, then dip in the saké and shoyu.   **(5–6)**
5. Arrange the salmon on a warmed plate, garnishing with the *shishi-togarashi* peppers. To add a touch of elegance to the arrangement, serve on a bed of pine needles, as shown in the photograph.

* This simple cooking technique also works well with other fish such as flatfish, yellowtail, sardines, mackerel and horse macherel. Squid and shrimp make tasty alternatives.

Crispy Flatfish
Karei no kara-age

This dish is really two in one. Filleting the fish in this way leaves the head and bones in one piece, so while the flesh is served in tender bite-sized pieces, the head and bones are deep-fried until deliciously crispy.

2 whole flatfish (dab), about 11 oz.
  (300 g) each*
5 tablespoons *katakuriko* or cornstarch
Vegetable oil for frying
GARNISHES:
  ½ cup grated *daikon* with chilli
    peppers (*momiji-oroshi*), see page 154
  4 *asatsuki* or green onions
  1 *sudachi* or lime, cut in half
Juice of 1 *sudachi* or lemon

1. Scrape off the fish scales with a knife. Insert the knife under the gill opening and detach the base of the gill cover. Gut the fish and remove the gills. Rinse and pat dry.   (1–2)
2. Cut each fish into 4 fillets and the head and bones part (five-piece cut). Holding the tail, lay the fish with the black skin upwards. Make a cut along the backbone from the tail towards the head.   (3)
3. Slice into both the left and the right side across the bones to make the flesh easier to remove. Insert the knife in the cut along the backbone and push gently until the flesh slides off in one piece.
4. Turn over and repeat. Slice each fillet into 1" (3 cm) slices.   (4–6)
5. Wrap the *katakuriko* in gauze or kitchen paper (see page 54) and pat the head and bones until coated. Heat the oil to 350°F (180°C) and deep-fry slowly for about 15 minutes. Drain.   (7)
6. Pat the fish slices with *katakuriko*. Deep-fry until crisp, then drain.   (8–9)
7. Place the head and bones on a plate and arrange the fish slices on top. Place the *momiji-oroshi,* finely chopped *asatsuki* and *sudachi* as garnishes in front of the fish. Allow guests to help themselves

to the fish, adding garnishes and sprinkling with *sudachi* juice to taste.

* Equally good substitutes include: halibut, sardines and horse macherel.

Yellowtail Teriyaki
Buri no teriyaki

Marinaded and then broiled, this oily yellowtail is glazed in a sweet, rich sauce.

4 slices yellowtail (or sea bream),
 about 4 oz. (120 g) each
MARINADE :
 ¼ cup saké
 ½ cup mirin
 ½ cup shoyu
 1 heaped tablespoon sugar
Mirin to glaze
GARNISHES:
 ⅔ cup grated *daikon*
 A little ginger *umezu-zuke**, minced
 3 tablespoons grated fresh root ginger
 ½ lemon, cut into half-moon slices
 (*hangetsu-giri*), see page 18

1. Mix the marinade in a shallow dish and add the fish. Let stand for about an hour, turning to ensure even coating. **(1)**
2. Preheat the oven to 480°F (250C°). Drain the fish, reserving the marinade for basting, and lay on a rack over a baking tray. Broil for 7–8 minutes or until the skin begins to brown. **(2)**
3. Using a brush, baste the fish 3 times with the marinade. Broil for 3 minutes. Baste the fish again, cover with aluminum foil and broil for a further 4–5 minutes. **(3–4)**
4. Drain the *daikon* lightly and mix with the minced ginger *umezu-zuke*. **(5)**
5. Brush with mirin to glaze, then transfer to a warmed plate. Arrange the *daikon*, grated ginger and *hangetsu-giri* lemon in front of the fish.

* Ginger *umezu-zuke* consists of thinly sliced ginger parboiled and soaked in sweetened plum vinegar (the sour liquid from salted *ume*). *Sudori-shoga* (see page 45) would make a good substitute.

Garnishes for Broiled Dishes
Yakimono no Ashirai

Salt-broiled dishes and teriyaki dishes are generally served with a vegetable garnish. Since it is only a small amount and is invariably placed

in front of the fish, it can be referred to either as *ashirai* (accompaniments) or *maemori* (garnishes in front). It serves to refresh the palate (*kuchinaoshi*) while also enhancing the flavors and colors of the dish.

Plain, vinegared and spicy vegetables all make good garnishes. Pickled ginger shoots (*sudori-shoga*), turnip in sweet vinegar, grated *daikon* with lemon, broiled *shishi-togarashi* peppers and *negi* are a few common examples.

Sometimes even sweet dishes, such as beans, kumquats or sour plums in syrup are served as garnishes.

Simmered Fish
Kinmedai no nitsuke

This dish of oily white fish in a broth both sweet and salty goes beautifully with its green vegetable garnish and plain steamed rice.

4 slices *kinmedai* or red sea bream, about 3½ oz. (100 g) each*
3½ oz. (100 g) *komatsu-na*
Dash of salt
SIMMERING STOCK:
  1 cup dashi stock or water
  2 tablespoons saké
  3½ tablespoons sugar
  3½ tablespoons mirin
  4 tablespoons shoyu

1. Blanch the *komatsu-na* in boiling water to turn it bright green. Then plunge it into cold water and squeeze out the excess water. Cut into 2″ (5 cm) lengths.
2. Bring the dashi or water to a boil in a saucepan. Add the other stock ingredients. Once the stock boils, place the fish, skin upwards, in the pan so the slices do not touch each other.   **(1)**
3. Ladle the stock over the fish.   **(2)**
4. Skim off any scum that forms. Cover with a wet drop lid (see page 148) or lay aluminum foil directly over the fish. Cook over medium heat for about 10 minutes.   **(3–5)**
5. Arrange the fish on a warmed plate. Dip the *komatsu-na* in the stock and arrange in front of the fish. Ladle stock over the dish.   **(6)**

* *Kinmedai* (alfonsino) is an oily white fish. If unavailable, flatfish, smelt, horse mackerel and sea bass make good substitutes.

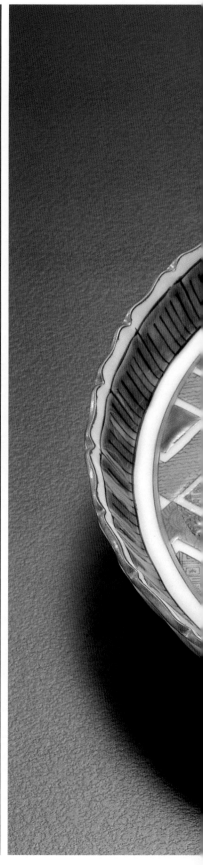

Tempura

A classic dish made from the freshest seafood and vegetables, coated in the lightest batter, and deep-fried until crisp. To keep the ingredients fresh and the batter crisp, prepare and cook as quickly as possible.

12 jumbo shrimp
11 oz. (300 g) squid (body)
12 fresh *shiitake* mushrooms
12 *shishi-togarashi* peppers
16 *shiso* leaves
Flour for coating
TEMPURA BATTER:
  1 lightly beaten egg mixed with
    cold water to make 1¼ cups
  1¼ cups all-purpose flour, sifted
Vegetable oil for deep-frying
TEMPURA SAUCE:
  ½ oz. (15 g) dried bonito flakes
  1 cup water
  ¼ cup mirin
  ¼ cup light shoyu
1 cup grated *daikon* to serve

1. Prepare the sauce first. Place all the ingredients for the sauce in a pan and bring to a boil over medium heat. Remove from heat and allow to cool. Strain.
2. Remove the heads from the shrimp. Shell and devein but leave the tails on. Cut out only the hard part from the center of the tail. Press tails with a knife to squeeze out excess liquid. Make 2–3 cuts on the undersides of the shrimp to prevent them from curling up during cooking. **(1–3)**
3. Peel the squid. Cut lengthwise into three and then crosswise into slices of approximately ¾" x 1½" (2 cm x 4 cm). Score each piece vertically twice. **(4)**
4. Wipe the caps of the *shiitake* mushrooms with a damp cloth. Cut off the stems. **(5)**
5. Wash the *shishi-togarashi* peppers and dry well. Trim the stems and make a slash down of each to prevent oil from spattering during cooking.

6. Wash the *shiso* leaves and dry well. Cut off the stems.

7. Start heating the oil gradually. While it is heating, prepare the batter. Mix the egg and cold water well. Add all the sifted flour at once and fold in only lightly with cooking chopsticks, as if drawing crosses in the batter. Add an ice cube. **(6–7)**

8. Transfer half of the batter to another bowl and refrigerate until needed. This prevents the mixture from becoming sticky.

9. Dip the tip of the chopsticks in the first batch of batter and drop a small amount into the hot oil. When it sinks halfway then immediately breaks up, the temperature has reached 350°F (180°C) and the oil is ready.

10. Dip the shrimp in flour, then dust off the excess. Dip in the batter and slide gently into the hot oil. Cook in small quantities, not allowing the shrimp to cover more than half of the surface of the oil. When the shrimp turn a crispy golden color, drain and place separately on a rack. Deep-fry the squid in the same way. **(8–9)**

11. When all the squid pieces have been cooked, turn off the heat to allow the temperature of the oil to fall slightly to about 340°F (170°C). Add the second batch of batter to the first. Turn the heat back on and deep-fry the *shiitake* mushrooms and *shishi-togarashi* peppers in the same way as the shrimp.

12. Lower the heat slightly. Dip the back of the *shiso* leaves in flour, then in batter. Place two leaves together and dip in the batter again. Deep-fry until crisp.

13. Arrange the tempura on a serving dish. Pour the tempura sauce into serving bowls and place a small mound of grated *daikon* in the center of each. Serve immediately. Dip the tempura in the sauce before eating.

* If using live prawns, deep-fry the heads without dipping in batter. Arrange as shown in the picture.

One-Pot Cooking
Nabemono

Japan boasts a great variety of *nabe-mono* (*nabe* for short), ranging from the simple Simmering Tofu (page 105) to the elaborate Sukiyaki (page 102). *Nabe* are especially popular in winter, when friends and family enjoy cooking and eating at the table.

To prepare a *nabe*, place a table-top burner in the center of the table and set a cast-iron skillet on top. An electric skillet or any portable stove with a temperature control makes a good substitute.
  Arrange the ingredients to be cooked attractively on a platter and put the garnishes, seasonings and dipping sauces in small serving dishes. Place on the table.
  Give each of the guests a small bowl so they can help themselves to sauces, garnishes and, of course, from the skillet. Keep replenishing the skillet, taking care that the heat is not too high and that the ingredients do not overcook. When making a well-flavored *nabe*, such as Seafood Stew, Table-Top Chicken, or Shabu-Shabu, don't throw the stock away at the end, but add cooked noodles, rice or *mochi* rice cakes. *Nabe* are meant to be enjoyed to the last drop!

Seafood Stew
Yosenabe

Cooked at the table, this is a real treat in cold weather, when the fish are at the peak of their flavor.

14 oz. (400 g) red sea bream or cod
3 boiled crab legs and 3 claws
12 oz. (300 g) oysters
1 cup grated *daikon*
3½ oz. (100 g) spinach
  Dash of salt
8 Chinese cabbage leaves
  Dash of salt
1½ lb. (600 g) *daikon*
1½ carrots, about 8 oz. (250 g)
8 fresh *shiitake* mushrooms
3 leeks
5 oz. (150 g) *seri* or watercress
1 block firm tofu
COOKING BROTH:
  8 cups dashi stock
  3 tablespoons saké
  1 slightly rounded tablespoon salt
  3 tablespoons light shoyu
Kabosu (or other sharp, tangy citrus fruit, e.g. *sudachi* or lemon) to serve

Bamboo mat
Flameproof casserole dish
Portable cooking stove

1. Cut the fish into 1½" (4 cm) squares. Slice the crab legs diagonally and cut the claws in half to make them easier to eat.
2. Place the oysters in a bowl, add the grated *daikon* and mix well. When the *daikon* turns brown, place the mixture in a colander and rinse briefly under running water. Drain well. **(1)**
3. Parboil the spinach in salted water. Plunge in cold water and squeeze out the excess water. Do the same with the Chinese cabbage. Drain in a colander.
4. Lay two Chinese cabbage leaves on the bamboo mat, the leafy parts overlapping in the center and the stalks facing out in opposite directions. Place ¼ of the spinach on top and roll up using

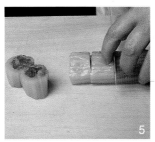

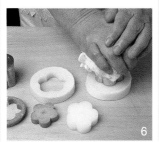

the bamboo mat. Then wrap the bamboo mat tightly around the vegetables and squeeze to remove excess liquid. Put an elastic band around the mat to set the shape of the roll and leave for 20 minutes. Cut into 1″ (3 cm) slices. Prepare the rest of the cabbage and spinach in the same way.   (2–5)

5. Cut 8 slices of *daikon* approximately ½″ (1 cm) wide. Use a vegetable cutter to cut into plum blossom shapes. Parboil and form into twisted plum blossoms (see page 19).   **(6)**

6. Cut the rest of the *daikon* into 1½″ (4 cm) strips. Blanch in boiling water, then plunge into cold water and drain. Cut some of the carrots into twisted plum blossoms and the rest into strips. Parboil and drain.

7. Wipe the caps of the *shiitake* mushrooms with a damp cloth and cut off the stems. Slice the leek diagonally. Cut the *seri* into 3″ (8 cm) lengths and the tofu into 1½″ (4 cm) squares.

8. Bring the dashi to a boil and add the other ingredients for the broth. Arrange the seafood, vegetables and tofu on a plate and place on the table.

9. Pour the liquid in the flameproof dish and bring to the table. Place on the portable cooking stove and bring to a boil. Add the various ingredients, a little at a time, and replenish the pot as needed. Start with the seafood (it flavors the stock) and any ingredients which require longer cooking. Give each guest a small bowl and allow them to help themselves from the pot. Sprinkle with *kabosu* juice to taste.

Seafood Stew➡

Chicken and Eggs

Chicken and Leek Kebabs
Yakitori

These mouth-watering kebabs, basted in a rich, fragrant sauce as they cook, are popular accompaniments to saké.

1 lb. (450 g) boned chicken thighs
  with the skin left on
2 leeks
BASTING SAUCE:
  ½ cup mirin
  ¼ cup shoyu
  2 heaped tablespoons sugar
Shichimi-togarashi to taste

Bamboo skewers, soaked in water for
  10 minutes to prevent scorching

1. Mix the ingredients for the basting sauce in a small saucepan. Cook over medium heat for 4–5 minutes to reduce. Set aside. **(1)**
2. Cut the chicken into 1–1½" (3 cm) cubes and the leek into 1" (2.5 cm) lengths. **(2–3)**
3. Thread the chicken and leek alternately onto skewers, starting and finishing each with a piece of chicken. **(4)**
4. Heat the oven to 475°F (250°C). Line a baking sheet with aluminum foil and lay the skewers on top. Cover the ends of the skewers with foil to prevent them from burning. **(5)**
5. Cook for 5 minutes, then remove the baking sheet from the oven. Holding three skewers at a time, spoon over the basting sauce. Turn as you spoon so that they are evenly coated. Repeat until all the kebabs are basted. **(6)**
6. Return to the oven for another 3 minutes. Remove and baste with sauce again. Cook for a final 3 minutes, then pour over the remaining sauce. Arrange the kebabs on a plate and serve immediately. Sprinkle with *shichimi-togarashi* to taste.

Chicken Teriyaki

Tori no nabe teriyaki

As the seasonings bubble down in the pan to a rich dark sauce, the glazed chicken turns golden-brown. Delicious with a vegetable garnish.

14 oz. (400 g) chicken thighs, boned but with skin left on
4 tablespoons *katakuriko* or cornstarch
1½ tablespoons vegetable oil
TERIYAKI SAUCE:
  3 tablespoons saké
  3 tablespoons sugar
  3 tablespoons shoyu
  2 tablespoons mirin
GARNISHES:
  1 red pepper
  1 green pepper
  1 yellow pepper
  1 tablespoon shoyu

1. Trim fat off the chicken. Cut the chicken pieces lengthwise in half, then diagonally into thin slices. **(1)**
2. Cut the peppers lengthwise in half. Remove the seeds and slice into thin strips.
3. Blanch the peppers in salted boiling water. Drain in a colander, then mix with the shoyu and salt.
4. Prepare a gauze pack of *katakuriko.* Heat the oil in a frying pan and remove from heat. Pat the chicken slices with *katakuriko* and add to the pan. **(2)**
5. Return to the heat. Cook the chicken over medium heat, shaking the pan gently until browned all over. Dab each piece with a paper towel to absorb excess fat. **(3–4)**
6. Mix the ingredients for the sauce and pour over the chicken. Cook over medium heat for 1–2 minutes, turning occasionally. Once the sauce thickens and the chicken becomes glazed, arrange on a dish. Garnish with the drained peppers. **(5–6)**

* If using a small frying pan, cook the chicken in two separate batches. Combine when adding the sauce.

Ginger Chicken Salad

Tori sasami no wafu sarada

This is a light and refreshing salad of shredded chicken on a mound of fresh vegetables and seaweed, served with a ginger dressing.

7–8 oz. (200–250 g) skinless chicken
  breasts
¼ teaspoon salt
3 tablespoons saké
Pinch of black pepper
8 oz. (200 g) *ogo-nori** or *wakame* seaweed
1 small cucumber, about 3½ oz. (100 g)
1/2 medium carrot
3½ oz. (100 g) *daikon* sprouts
GINGER DRESSING:
  1–2 teaspoons ginger juice*
  2 tablespoons vinegar
  2 tablespoons light shoyu
  2 tablespoons dashi
GARNISH:
  Beni-tade

1. Mix the ingredients for the dressing and refrigerate.
2. Slice the chicken into 12 slices. **(1)**
3. Place the chicken in a pan and sprinkle with salt and saké. Cover tightly with a drop lid or aluminum foil with a hole in the center and simmer over a low heat until the liquid has completely evaporated. **(2)**
4. Remove the chicken from the pan and allow to cool. Shred finely along the grain of the meat. **(3)**
5. Rinse the *ogo-nori* and drain well in a colander. Cut into bite-sized pieces.
6. Rub the cucumber lightly with salt. Blanch in boiling water, then plunge into cold water until it turns bright green. Cut into 1" (3 cm) julienne strips. Cut the carrot into strips of the same length.
7. Rinse the *daikon* sprouts and cut off the base. Cut the stems in half.
8. Soak the *ogo-nori* and vegetables in ice water for about 10 minutes, then drain well in a colander. Heap on serving plates and arrange the shredded ➤

Green Fried Chicken

Tori sasami no wakakusa-age

This dish gets its unusual color from a powdered seaweed called *aonoriko*. For a variation in flavor, try green *shiso* or parsley instead.

12 oz. (350 g) skinless chicken breast
1 tablespoon saké
⅓ teaspoon salt
2 tablespoons *katakuriko* or cornstarch
BATTER:
  ½ beaten egg
  Just over ½ cup water
  ¾ cup flour

➤ chicken on top. Garnish with *beni-tade*. Serve with chilled ginger dressing.

* *Ogo-nori* is a form of seaweed.
* To make ginger juice, wrap grated ginger in a slightly damp cloth and squeeze out the juice.

2 tablespoons *aonoriko*
Vegetable oil for deep-frying
GARNISH:
  12 boiled broad beans

1. Cut the chicken into 20 thin slices and sprinkle with the saké and salt. Let stand for about 5 minutes, then pat with a gauze pack of *katakuriko*.   **(1)**
2. Mix the egg and the water in a bowl. Sift in the flour and sprinkle the *aonoriko* on top. Fold in lightly—do not overmix.   **(2)**
3. Heat the oil to about 340°F (170°C). Dip the chicken in the batter and gently drop into the hot oil, a little at a time. Cook for 1-2 minutes. Remove and drain on a wire rack over a shallow dish. Repeat.   **(3)**
4. Line a dish with absorbent paper and arrange the chicken on it. Garnish in front with the boiled broad beans.

Braised Chicken Balls and Turnips

Tori dango to kabu no nimono

These meatballs are made from such finely ground chicken and vegetables that they melt in your mouth. Served together with turnip and *wakame*, this is a very healthy and mild-tasting dish.

CHICKEN BALLS:

11 oz. (300 g) skinless chicken ground twice until smooth
½ beaten egg
3 tablespoons grated onion
3 tablespoons finely chopped cloud ear mushroom
3 tablespoons finely chopped carrot
1 tablespoon sugar
½ tablespoon light shoyu
6 small turnips, each about 3½ oz. (100 g)
¼ oz. (10 g) *wakame*, soaked in warm water and drained (unsoaked weight)

SIMMERING STOCK:

3 cups dashi stock
3 tablespoons saké
3 tablespoons mirin
3 tablespoons light shoyu
⅕ teaspoon salt

GARNISH:

3–4 strips *yuzu* peel, each measuring ⅓" x ¾" (8 mm x 2 cm), made into "pine needle *yuzu*", see page 19

1. Using your hands, mix together all the ingredients for the chicken balls except the cloud ear mushroom and the carrot. Knead until sticky. Add the cloud ear mushroom, the carrot and a dash of salt. **(1–2)**

2. Bring to a boil 5 cups of water in a medium-sized saucepan. Form the mixture into 1" (3 cm) balls and drop into the boiling water one at a time. Boil for 2 minutes or until the outside turns whitish. Drain, soak briefly in cold water to rinse off the excess oil, then drain in a colander. **(3–4)**

3. Trim the turnip leaves, leaving about ¾" (2 cm) of the stalk for color. Wash the dirt from the base of the stalks. Peel the turnips and cut in half lengthwise.

4. Place the turnips in a pan of salted water and bring to a boil. The turnips are done when a bamboo skewer can easily be inserted. Place in cold water to cool, then drain in a colander. **(5)**

5. Dip the soaked *wakame* into boiling water, then plunge into cold water. Squeeze out excess water and cut into 1" (2–3 cm) lengths.

6. Bring the dashi to a boil and add the other ingredients for the stock. Add the chicken balls and cover with a drop lid or with aluminum foil. Cook over medium heat for 5–6 minutes, then remove the chicken balls. **(6)**

7. Add the turnips to the stock and cover again with the drop lid or aluminum foil. Cook for 7–8 minutes over medium heat. Lower the heat and add the chicken balls. Continue to cook for about 2–3 minutes or until heated through. **(7)**

8. Arrange the turnips and chicken balls in warmed dishes. Dip the *wakame* in the stock and add. Ladle over a little stock and scatter "pine needle *yuzu*" on top. **(8)**

Table-Top Chicken
Tori no mizutaki

Another *nabe* (one-pot dish) simmered and eaten at the table. This one, however, is pre-cooked to make the chicken tender. It continues to simmer at the table as guests help themselves to the mild chicken and the tangy sauce. Later, add a little salt to the stock and serve it as soup or use as stock for cooking *udon* noodles.

2 lbs. 4 oz. (1 kg) chicken meat with
  bones, roughly chopped into 2½"
  (6 cm) chunks
SIMMERING STOCK:
  10 cups water
  ½ cup saké
1 head lettuce
CONDIMENTS:
  ½–1 cup minced *asatsuki* or chives
  ½–1 cup grated *daikon* with chilli
    peppers (*momiji-oroshi*), see page 154
Ponzu sauce to taste, see page 17

Flameproof casserole dish
Tabletop burner

1. Rinse the chicken, then place it in a colander and pour boiling water over it. Rinse again to remove impurities and fat. **(1–2)**
2. Place the chicken in a pan and add water. Bring to a boil over high heat. Turn down the heat, skim fat from the surface and add the saké. Simmer for about 1 hour. Do not cover as this makes the stock cloudy. **(3–5)**
3. Wash the lettuce. Cut large leaves lengthwise into 2 or 3 pieces. Shred finely.
4. Transfer the chicken to the casserole dish once tender. Strain and add the stock. Place the casserole on the table-top burner and start to heat. **(6)**
5. Add the lettuce a little at a time. Allow guests to help themselves to the chicken, condiments and the *ponzu* sauce.

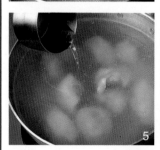

Rolled Eggs

Tamago-yaki san-shu

These light omelets are seasoned with dashi, sugar, mirin or shoyu and rolled into delicate bite-size shapes. As each varies slightly in flavor, shape and shade, they can be combined to make an elegant, unusual arrangement.

Gourd-Shaped Eggs

Hisago Tamago

5 eggs
SEASONINGS:
  2½ tablespoons sugar
  ½ tablespoon mirin
  1 teaspoon light shoyu
  Dash of salt
Vegetable oil

Japanese omelet pan (or skillet)
Bamboo mat

1. Stir the eggs but do not beat. "Cut" through the egg whites by lifting them up 3 or 4 times with cooking chopsticks. Add the seasonings and mix. Strain through a sieve.
2. Heat a 7" (18 cm) square omelet pan and wipe the surface well with an oiled paper towel. Reduce the heat to medium and pour in ⅓ of the egg mixture. **(1–2)**
3. When the egg is half-set, use cooking chopsticks to ensure that all four corners are free from the pan. Fold the egg into three, starting from the back of the pan. Wipe the skillet again with oil. Slide the folded egg towards the back of the pan and wipe the rest of the pan with oil. Pour in half of the remaining egg mixture, spreading it evenly over the pan. Bring the rolled egg into this second omelet and fold over towards the front of the pan. Add the remainder of the egg and repeat. Roll the cooked egg up in a bamboo mat immediately. **(3–7)**
4. To shape, press the mat gently along

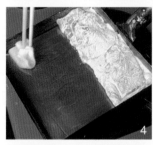

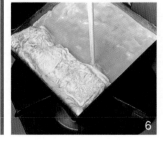

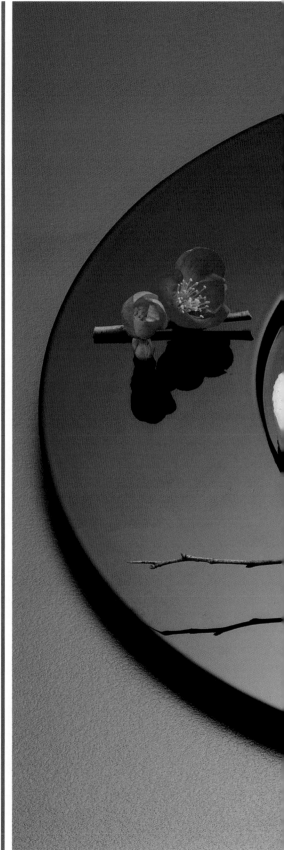

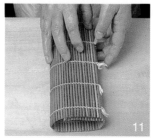

its length with your fingers, so that the slight indentation divides the egg roll into a proportion of ⅓ to ⅔. Let set for 10 minutes. Slice the roll into bite-size widths before serving. **(8–10)**

* If using a round skillet, trim the ends of the omelet after rolling it up.

Rolled Eggs with Dashi
Dashi-maki tamago

4 eggs
SEASONINGS:
  ½ cup dashi stock
  ⅔ tablespoon light shoyu
  Dash of salt
Vegetable oil

Japanese omelet pan (or skillet)
Bamboo mat

1. Mix the eggs and seasonings gently and strain through a sieve.
2. Heat a 7" (18 cm) square omelet pan and wipe the surface well with an oiled paper towel. Reduce the heat to medium and pour in ⅓ of the egg mixture.
3. When the egg is half-set, use cooking chopsticks to ensure that the corners are not stuck. Fold the egg into three, starting from the back of the pan. Oil the pan again. Slide the folded egg towards the back of the pan and wipe the rest of the pan with oil. Pour in half of the remaining egg mixture, spreading it evenly over the pan. Fold the rolled egg in and continue to fold towards the front of the pan. Add the remainder of the egg and repeat.
4. Once cooked, transfer immediately to a bamboo mat. Roll up from both ends. Leave for 10 minutes for the shape to set, then cut into slices. **(11)**

Rolled Eggs with Spinach
Ao-na-maki Tamago

4 eggs
SEASONINGS:
  2 tablespoons sugar
  Dash of salt
4 stalks cooked spinach
2 teaspoons light shoyu
Vegetable oil

Japanese omelet pan (or skillet)
Bamboo mat

1. Stir the eggs gently with the seasonings and strain.
2. Remove the spinach roots. Lay the spinach out with two stems facing one way, two stems facing the other. Sprinkle with the light shoyu, leave for about 5 minutes, then squeeze gently.
3. Heat the pan and wipe the surface with oil. Pour in ⅓ of the egg mixture. When half-set, lay the spinach across the eggs towards the back. Roll the egg towards you, enclosing the spinach. Add the remainder of the egg as in the preceding recipes. **(12)**
4. Roll the egg in a bamboo mat. Leave to rest for about 10 minutes before cutting into slices.

Savory Steamed Custard

Chawanmushi

Colorful and tasty morsels lie hidden under this light, savory custard. Its subtle flavor and smooth texture make it a good substitute for soup in a Japanese-style meal.

8 oz. (250 g) skinless chicken breasts
1 teaspoon salt
1 teaspoon saké
3 dried *shiitake* mushrooms
4 slices each of red and white *kamaboko*
8 pieces *ume-fu*, soaked
12 shelled gingko nuts, boiled and
   skinned
SAVORY CUSTARD:
   3 eggs
   3 cups dashi stock
   1 teaspoon salt
   1 teaspoon saké
   1 teaspoon light shoyu
   ½ teaspoon sugar
GARNISH:
   12 stalks *mitsuba*
   4 strips *yuzu* peel, each ¾" x ¼"
     (2 cm x 8 mm), made into "pine
     needle *yuzu*", see page 19

4 *chawanmushi* dishes*
Steamer

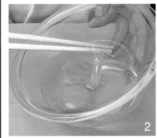

1. Rinse the *shiitake* mushrooms and soak until soft in water to cover. Cut off the stems and dice the mushrooms into cubes of about ½" (5–6 mm).   **(1)**
2. Cut the chicken into thin slices. Sprinkle with saké and light shoyu. Blanch the *ume-fu* in boiling water.
3. Break the eggs in a bowl. Use the cooking chopsticks to lift up the egg whites three or four times. This mixes the eggs without beating air into them. Add the remaining ingredients for the custard and mix well. Strain.   **(2–5)**
4. Place the chicken and *shiitake* in the *chawanmushi* dishes. Divide the custard between the four dishes, but reserve 5 tablespoons of the mixture.   **(6)**
5. Place the water in the steamer, cover and bring to the boil. Once it is full of steam, place the dishes inside. Cover and steam over high heat for 1 minute, then over low heat for 16–17 minutes.   **(7)**
6. When the surface of the custard sets, divide the red and white *kamaboko,* gingko nuts and *ume-fu* between the dishes. Pour over the remaining custard mixture and cook for a further 2–3 minutes.   **(8–9)**
7. Cut the *mitsuba* into 1½" (3–4 cm) lengths. Make each *yuzu* strip into "pine needle *yuzu*." When the custards are lightly set, garnish each with the *mitsuba* and "pine needle *yuzu*." Cover and serve with a teaspoon.

* *Chawanmushi* dishes are small but deep china bowls with lids. If you do not have *chawanmushi* dishes, use any heat-resistant bowls or cups (as shown in the photograph). However, the delicate consistency of this dish makes it necessary to use individual dishes rather than a single large serving dish.

➧Savory Steamed Custard

Steak Japanese Style
Wafu steak

This is steak with a difference, both in the seasoning and the way of serving. Remember: to be eaten with chopsticks, steak must be bite-sized!

1 sirloin steak, about 12 oz. (350 g) and 1" (2 cm) thick*
Dash of salt and pepper
¾–1 oz. (20–30 g) beef suet
1 tablespoon saké
2 tablespoons shoyu
1 cup grated *daikon* with minced *bofu* stalks
GARNISH:
 Bofu or watercress

1. Sprinkle the steak with salt and pepper and gently pat it all over. **(1)**
2. Melt the fat in a frying pan over low heat. Turn up the heat and add the steak. Shaking the frying pan gently, sear one side of the meat over high heat. Turn over and repeat with the other side. Remove from heat and sprinkle with the saké and shoyu. **(2–5)**
3. Cut the steak into 1½" (4 cm) squares and arrange on a serving dish. Reduce the juices in the frying pan for 10 seconds and pour over the steak. Place a mound of grated *daikon* and minced *bofu* in front of the steak. Garnish with a sprig of *bofu*. **(6–7)**

* To increase the number of servings, cook additional pieces of meat rather than one larger cut to ensure even cooking.

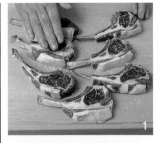

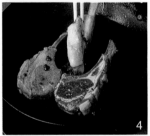

Spicy Lamb Chops
Hone-tsuki ramu no sansho-yaki

The peppery bite of *mi-zansho* adds a piquancy to this dish which balances the strong flavor of the lamb.

12 lamb rib chops
Dash of salt and pepper
3 tablespoons vegetable oil
MARINADE:
   4 tablespoons saké
   4 tablespoons shoyu
   2 tablespoons *mi-zansho no tsukudani* or capers
SIMMERING STOCK:
   1 cup dashi stock
   1 teaspoon saké
   Dash of salt
GARNISHES:
   4-8 pieces *temari-fu**
   Japanese paper and *mizuhiki* paper strings* or Western paper frills

1. Preheat the oven to 480°F (250°C).
2. Rub the lamb with the salt and pepper. Let stand for 5 minutes. **(1)**
3. Mix the marinade in a shallow dish. Chop the *mi-zansho no tsukudani* and add. Marinade the lamb for 5 minutes, turning it over occasionally. **(2–3)**
4. Heat the oil in a frying pan. Drain the lamb, reserving the marinade. Sear both sides of each chop over medium to high heat and remove from heat. **(4)**
5. Lay the lamb on a rack placed over a baking sheet and sprinkle with the reserved *mi-zansho no tsukudani.* Roast for 7 minutes. **(5)**
6. Place the *temari-fu* in a saucepan and pour over just enough water to cover it. Simmer for about one minute, then drain and refill with the simmering stock. Simmer over low heat for 3 minutes, then remove from heat.
7. Wrap the end of each chop with Japanese paper and tie with *mizuhiki* in a decorative knot. Arrange on warmed plates and garnish with *temari-fu.*

* *Temari-fu* is wheat gluten (*fu*) in the shape

of a *temari* ball, a traditional girls' toy. *Temari* are made by winding colored thread around a cotton center.
* *Mizuhiki* paper strings are used for tying decorative knots. Made from Japanese paper, they are shredded, twisted and glued together.

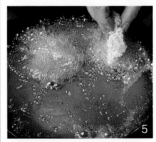

Crispy Pork Cutlets
Ton-katsu or *hire-katsu*

This succulent pork in a crispy coating is served with a piquant *ton-katsu* sauce and a mound of finely shredded cabbage. The recipe uses tenderloin (*hire*) instead of the more usual loin.

1 lb. 6 oz. (600 g) pork tenderloin*
Dash of salt and pepper
TO COAT:
  Flour
  2 eggs, beaten
  Breadcrumbs
Vegetable oil for deep-frying
TON-KATSU SAUCE:
  ½ cup Worcestershire sauce
  2 tablespoons shoyu
  1–2 tablespoons tomato ketchup
GARNISHES:
  6 leaves cabbage
  3 radishes
  4 "half-moon" (*hangetsu-giri*) lemon
    slices, see page 18
Mustard to taste

1. Cut the pork into ¾" (2 cm) slices. Sprinkle with salt and pepper. **(1)**
2. Dredge the pork slices with flour and pat off the excess. Dip in the egg, then the breadcrumbs and refrigerate for 30 minutes. **(2–3)**
3. Cut out the hard stalk of the cabbage leaves and slice each leaf lengthwise in half. Layer three pieces together, roll up tightly and slice into fine threads. Soak the cabbage threads in cold water. **(4)**
4. Cut the radish into thin slices, then into fine strips. Soak in cold water with the cabbage. Once crisp, drain in a colander. Mix the ingredients for the sauce.
5. Heat the oil to 350°F (180°C). Add the pork, turning when it becomes golden and crispy. Continue to cook for 5–6 minutes or until golden-brown. Drain well. **(5–6)**
6. Heap generous servings of cabbage onto plates and arrange the pork in

front. Garnish with lemon and mustard. Serve sauce on the side.

* If using loin, each serving should be approximately 4 oz. (120 g). Dip the slices in the coating and cook as above. After draining, cut each slice into bite-size pieces and reassemble on the serving plates.

Braised Beef and Potatoes
Nikujaga

The secret of a good *nikujaga* is to stew the beef and potatoes together until the potatoes have absorbed the flavor of the meat.

11 oz. (300 g) thinly sliced beef with
   any fat left on
1¾ lb. (800 g) potatoes
11 oz. (300 g) onions
½ tablespoon vegetable oil
SIMMERING STOCK:
  Dashi stock, as needed
  3 tablespoons saké
  6 tablespoons sugar
  2 tablespoons mirin
  5 tablespoons shoyu
GARNISH:
  2 tablespoons green peas, cooked

1. Cut the beef into 2–2½" (5–6 cm) lengths, separating the slices well.
2. Peel the potatoes and cut into quarters. Soak in cold water, then rinse and drain in a colander. **(1)**
3. Peel the onion and cut lengthwise in half. Cut into ½" (5–6 mm) slices.
4. Heat a saucepan and add the oil. Remove from heat and cool slightly. Add the beef, separating it with chopsticks. **(2)**
5. Return the pan to the heat and brown the beef. Add the onions, then the potatoes. **(3)**
6. Once the meat and vegetables have absorbed the oil, pour over just enough dashi to cover them. Add the rest of the stock ingredients and turn up the heat. **(4)**
7. Bring the mixture to a boil, skimming off any scum that forms. Reduce the heat slightly. Skim off remaining scum and cover with a drop lid (see page 24) or aluminum foil. **(5–6)**
8. As the stock reduces, shake the pan a few times to coat the meat and vegetables evenly. **(7)**

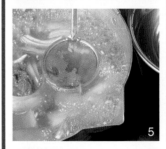

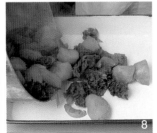

9. When almost all the stock has been absorbed, remove from heat and transfer to a serving dish. Serve in small bowls and sprinkle with the cooked green peas.   (8)

Shabu-Shabu

The name of this famous dish comes from the sound the beef makes as you swish it around the pot of bubbling water with your chopsticks. Once the beef is cooked, dip it in either a tangy vinegar-based sauce or a creamy sesame sauce. One tip: cut the vegetables thinly so that they cook faster.

1½ lbs. (600 g) paper-thin slices of beef
4 leaves Chinese cabbage
2 leeks
8 fresh *shiitake* mushrooms
7 oz. (200 g) watercress
3½ oz. (100 g) *harusame*
SESAME SAUCE:
   4 tablespoons sesame paste
      (*atari-goma*)
   3 tablespoons sugar
   2 tablespoons miso
   2 tablespoons shoyu
   2 tablespoons saké
   6 tablespoons Japanese rice vinegar
   1 tablespoon sesame oil
   Dash of *shichimi-togarashi*
VINEGAR SAUCE:
   ½ cup vinegar
   ½ cup light shoyu
   ½ cup dashi stock

Earthenware pot or cast-iron skillet
Tabletop burner

1. Cut the Chinese cabbage leaves and stalks separately into thin strips about 2″ x ½″ (1 cm x 1 cm). **(1)**
2. Cut the leeks the same length as the Chinese cabbage, then slice lengthwise into two or three strips. Wipe the caps of the *shiitake* mushrooms and cut off the stems. Cut the watercress into 2″ (5 cm) lengths. **(2–3)**
3. Soak the *harusame* in boiling water. When it turns transparent, drain and soak in cold water. Drain and cut into 4″ (10 cm) lengths. **(4–5)**
4. Mix the two sauces separately and pour into serving dishes.
5. Arrange the vegetables on a serving platter. Folding each slice of beef in half, arrange in the foreground. Place the meat, vegetables and sauces on the table.
6. Place a skillet on the tabletop burner and pour in boiling water. Once the water returns to the boil, guests can start to cook their own beef. Swish a slice of beef around in the water a couple of times with your chopsticks, taking it out as soon as it changes color. Dip in one of the two sauces before eating. Gradually add the vegetables and *harusame,* a little at a time, skimming off any scum as it forms.

Sukiyaki

Consisting of tender beef and vegetables braised at the table in a cast-iron skillet and dipped in raw egg, this is probably the most famous of all Japanese dishes.

1½ lbs. (600 g) paper-thin slices of beef
1 oz. (30 g) beef suet
5 leeks
7–11 oz. (200–300 g) *shirataki*
1 block grilled tofu (*yaki-dofu*)
7–11 oz. (200–300 g) *shungiku*
BROTH:
  Sugar, saké, mirin and shoyu as required
TO SERVE:
  4–8 eggs

Sukiyaki skillet or casserole dish
Tabletop burner

1. Cut the leeks diagonally into thin slices.   (1)
2. Parboil the *shirataki* for 5 minutes. Drain and soak in cold water. Squeeze out the excess water and cut the threads into thirds or quarters to make them easier to eat.   (2–3)
3. Cut the grilled tofu lengthwise in half, then crosswise into pieces about 1½″ (3.5 cm) wide.   (4)
4. Pull the leafy stems off the *shungiku*, discarding the hard stalks.
5. Arrange the meat and other ingredients on a large serving platter. Put the eggs in a separate dish. Take the dishes and seasonings to the table.
6. Heat the sukiyaki skillet on the cooking stove. Add the beef suet and melt over a low heat.   (5)
7. Add ⅓ of the leeks and sauté over a low heat until fragrant. Add ⅓ of the beef, one slice at a time. Turn and sprinkle with 3 tablespoons each of sugar, saké and mirin and 2 tablespoons of shoyu. Each guest takes an egg, breaks it in a bowl and lightly beats it. When the food is cooked, they help themselves, dipping it in the egg before eating.   (6–8)
7. Add the rest of the leeks and beef. Then add the *shirataki*, grilled tofu and *shungiku*, a little at a time. As the broth boils down, replenish with hot water and season to taste.

Chilled Tofu

Hiyayakko

Chilled and served with assorted garnishes and shoyu, this must be the simplest tofu dish to prepare, yet also among the most delicious. A perfect supper dish for a hot summer evening.

2 blocks "silken" tofu, each approx.
  10 oz. (300 g)
GARNISHES:
  ¼ Japanese cucumber
    Dash of salt
  4–5 baby cucumbers with flowers
    (or other small green leaf garnish)
    Dash of salt
CONDIMENTS:
  20 green *shiso* leaves
  1" (2.5 cm) piece of fresh ginger root
  3 *myoga* shoots
  Shoyu to serve

1. Cut the ¼ cucumber into slices 1" (2.5 cm) thick. Hollow out each sliceusing a corer and discard the flesh. Slice the cucumber thinly. Rinse with boiling water and dip in cold water immediately.   **(1)**
2. Rub the baby cucumbers lightly with salt. Rinse and trim the ends.
3. Cut the *shiso* leaves in half. Layer five pieces at a time and roll up lengthwise. Slice the rolls finely. Soak briefly in cold water, then squeeze out the excess water.   **(2–3)**
4. Thinly peel the ginger and grate finely. Slice the *myoga* thinly.
5. Half-fill a glass serving bowl with cold water. Cut the tofu into 1½" (4 cm) cubes and place in the bowl. Add ice cubes, cucumber rings and baby cucumbers.
6. Serve guests with a small plate of shoyu into which they can mix the various garnishes. Serve the tofu onto the plates with a slotted spoon.

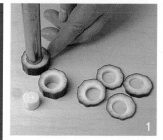

Simmering Tofu

Yudofu

For this effortless *nabe* (one-pot dish), tofu is heated at the table only until warmed through and served with simple condiments.

2 blocks "silken" tofu, each approx. 10 oz. (300 g)
1 piece *kombu*, 7½" (20 cm) in length
½ *negi* or 2 green onions
1 cup bonito flakes
Shoyu to serve

Casserole dish or earthenware pot
Tabletop burner

1. Wipe both sides of the *kombu* with a dry cloth to remove dirt. Lay the *kombu* on the bottom of a casserole dish or earthenware pot and fill with water. Let stand for 30 minutes to soften.
2. To mince the *negi* finely, first cut lengthwise 4-6 times, then slice thinly crosswise. **(1–2)**
3. Cut the block of tofu in half lengthwise, then cut into 2" (4 cm) cubes.
4. Place the pan on the tabletop burner and heat gently. When the water begins to boil, add some of the tofu. Cook only until it starts to sway in the water. As it is easy to overcook tofu, cook only a little at a time. Serve guests with small plates of shoyu and allow them to add *negi* and bonito flakes according to taste. Serve tofu onto the plates with a slotted spoon.

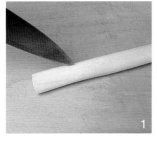

Deep-Fried Tofu
Agedashi-dofu

Deep-fried until crisp on the outside and creamy on the inside, the tofu is served with plenty of condiments and a delicious sauce. The secret is to serve it immediately.

1 block "silken" tofu, approx. 10 oz. (300 g)
3 tablespoons *katakuriko* (or cornstarch)
Vegetable oil for deep-frying
FOR THE SAUCE:
  1 cup dashi stock
  1 tablespoon saké
  3 tablespoons light shoyu
  1 teaspoon mirin
GARNISHES:
  4 rounded tablespoons grated *daikon* with chilli peppers (*momiji-oroshi*), see page 154
  6 *asatsuki* or 3 green onions
  Just under 1 cup bonito flakes

1. Wrap the tofu in a kitchen cloth. Refrigerate for 30 minutes to allow it to drain. Cut into quarters. **(1)**
2. Mix the ingredients for the sauce in a small saucepan and set aside. Slice the *asatsuki* finely and set aside.
3. Heat the oil to 340°F (175°C). Pat the sides of the tofu gently with a gauze pack of *katakuriko*. Gently slide the tofu into the hot oil. **(3)**
4. Deep-fry slowly until the tofu starts to change color and become crisp. Remove and leave to drain on a wire rack set over a shallow dish. Place in serving dishes. **(4–5)**
5. Arrange the *momiji-oroshi*, *asatsuki* and bonito flakes on top of the tofu and pour the sauce around the sides.

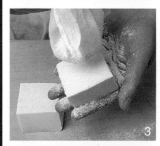

Konnyaku and Carrot Salad in Tofu Dressing
Konnyaku to ninjin no shira-ae

Ground sesame and tofu are blended into a creamy dressing for this traditional and nutritious dish.

7 oz. (200 g) *konnyaku*
4 dried *shiitake* mushrooms
2 oz. (50 g) carrots
1 Japanese cucumber
Salted water (1 teaspoon of salt to each cup of water)
DRESSING:
  1 block "cotton" tofu, approx. 10 oz. (300 g)
  6 tablespoons freshly toasted white sesame seeds
  3 tablespoons sugar
  1 tablespoon saké
  1 tablespoon light shoyu
  Dash of salt
SIMMERING STOCK:
  ½ cup dashi stock
  2 tablespoons mirin
  1 tablespoon light shoyu
GARNISH:
  Ginger *umezu-zuke,* see page 66

1. Blanch the tofu in boiling water. Drain and wrap in cloth, then roll in a bamboo mat. Sandwich between two chopping boards. Tilt the boards slightly and leave to drain for 30 minutes.
2. Place the *konnyaku* in water and bring to the boil. After 5 minutes, drain, soak in cold water and drain again. Slice the *konnyaku* horizontally into a top and a bottom half, then cut in half lengthwise. Slice finely.
3. Soak the *shiitake* mushrooms in water to soften. Squeeze out the excess water, cut off the stems and slice finely.
4. Cut the carrot into julienne strips about 1" x ¼" (3 cm x 5 mm).
5. Mix the ingredients for the stock and bring to a boil. Add the *konnyaku, shiitake* mushrooms and carrots. Simmer over medium heat until the liquid has

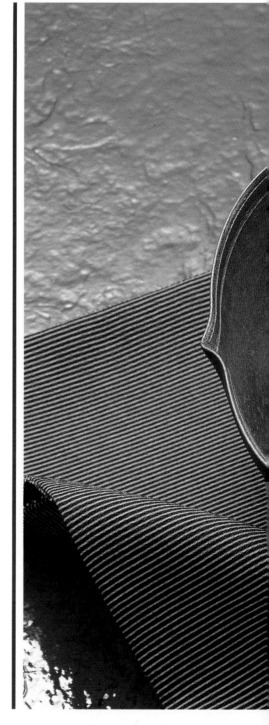

been absorbed. Remove from heat and place in a colander to cool. Refrigerate until ready to serve. **(1)**
6. Thinly slice the cucumber and soak in salted water until soft. Squeeze out excess water.
7. Grind the sesame seeds with a pestle

and mortar or food processor until oil appears in the mixture. Pass the tofu through a fine sieve and add to the sesame mixture. Mix well. Add the seasonings and continue to blend until the dressing is smooth and creamy. Refrigerate until ready to serve. **(2–4)**

8. To serve, mix the vegetables and the cucumber with the tofu dressing. Heap into serving bowls and garnish with the chopped pickled ginger.

Mushrooms and *Shungiku* in Tofu-Walnut Dressing

Kinoko to shungiku no shira-ae

With three different kinds of mushrooms and a touch of green in a well-flavored dressing, this dish is especially good for vegetarians and the health-conscious.

3½ oz. (100 g) *shimeji* mushrooms
3 fresh *shiitake* mushrooms
3½ oz. (100 g) *enoki* mushrooms
3½ oz. (100 g) *shungiku*
Dash of salt
½ tablespoon light shoyu
TOFU-WALNUT DRESSING:
  1 block "cotton" tofu, approx. 10 oz.
    (300 g)
  10 walnuts
  4 tablespoons sugar
  1 tablespoon saké
  1 tablespoon light shoyu
  Dash of salt
SIMMERING STOCK:
  3 tablespoons dashi stock
  2 tablespoons mirin
  1 tablespoon light shoyu
GARNISH:
  1 tablespoon sieved egg yolk,
    see page 46

1. Sieve the tofu (see page 109, #7).
2. Remove the ends of the *shimeji* mushrooms and break the mushrooms into smaller clumps. Cut off the stems of the *shiitake* mushrooms. Slice the mushrooms thinly.
3. Remove the ends of the *enoki* mushrooms, cut the stems in half and break the mushrooms into smaller clumps. Blanch in boiling water and drain.
4. Mix the ingredients for the simmering stock and bring to a boil. Add all the mushrooms. Simmer over medium heat until all the liquid has been absorbed. Place in a colander until cool, then refrigerate until needed. **(1)**
5. Cut off the ends of the *shungiku* and

blanch in salted boiling water. Dip in cold water and squeeze out the excess water. Cut into 1" (3 cm) lengths, sprinkle with light shoyu and refrigerate until needed. **(2)**
6. Soak walnuts in hot water. When the water cools, remove the thin skins. Chop the nuts roughly and grind in a

pestle and mortar or food processor.
Set aside. (3)
7. Grind the sieved tofu using the pestle
and mortar. Add the walnuts, then the
seasonings and continue to grind until
creamy. Refrigerate until serving.
8. To serve, mix the mushrooms and
the lightly drained *shungiku* in the tofu
dressing. Heap in serving bowls and
sprinkle with sieved egg yolk. (4)

Eggs in Tofu-Puff Purses
Fukuro-ni

Sheets of *aburage* are made into little purses containing boiled eggs. This is a quick and easy side dish.

3 sheets *aburage*
6 eggs
6 strips *kampyo*, each approx. 7" (15 cm) long, washed and rubbed with 1 teaspoon salt
SIMMERING STOCK:
  2 cups dashi stock
  1 tablespoon saké
  1½ tablespoons sugar
  1½ tablespoons mirin
  1½ tablespoons shoyu
GARNISH:
  3½ oz. (100 g) *daikon* sprouts, washed with ends trimmed off
Mustard to taste

1. Place the *aburage* on a chopping board and roll a cooking chopstick up and down its length. This separates the top layer from the bottom and makes it easier to open. Place the *aburage* in a colander and pour boiling water over it to rinse off excess oil. Cut each sheet crosswise in half. Carefully open up each half into a pouch. **(1–2)**

2. Immerse the *kampyo* in boiling water, then plunge immediately into cold water.

3. Break the eggs one at a time and place one in each *aburage* purse. Tie the neck of each purse securely with a strip of *kampyo*. **(3)**

4. Plunge the *daikon* sprouts into boiling water, then into cold water. Squeeze out the excess water.

5. Mix the ingredients for the simmering stock and bring to a boil. Line up the purses in the pan and return to a boil. Reduce the heat and cover with a drop lid. Simmer over low heat for ➤

Braised Tofu Puffs and Greens

Ao-na to aburage no nibitashi

Strips of *aburage* braised in a broth to which leafy greens are added. This is real home cooking!

2 sheets *aburage*
7 oz. (200 g) *komatsu-na*
  Dash of salt
SIMMERING STOCK:
  1½ cups dashi stock
  1 tablespoon saké
  1 tablespoon mirin
  2 tablespoons light shoyu
  ¼ teaspoon salt

➤ 20 minutes.

6. Heap in serving bowls and garnish with the *daikon* sprouts. Pour the stock over and serve with mustard on the side.

1. Put the *aburage* in a colander and pour boiling water over it to rinse off the oil. Cut lengthwise in half and slice thinly.   (1)
2. Cut off the roots of the *komatsu-na* and wash. Score any thick stalks lengthwise.
3. Bring a large pot of water to a boil and add salt. Blanch ⅓ of the *komatsu-na* at a time, dipping it immediately in cold water. Squeeze out the excess water and cut into ¾–1" (2–3 cm) lengths.
4. Combine the ingredients for the simmering stock in a large saucepan and bring to a boil. Add the *aburage* and simmer over medium heat for 1–2 minutes. Scatter the *komatsu-na* over the broth and continue to cook only until heated through.   (2–3)

Japanese Salad
Wafu Sarada

This is a delicious salad of colorful vegetables and fresh seafood. The miso adds an unusual piquancy to the dressing. Although the salad is Japanese, the dressing is called *nanbanzu* (Southern Barbarian Dressing) as *shichimi-togarashi* contains chilli pepper, a spice introduced by foreign traders.

7 oz. (200 g) *daikon*
1 oz. (30 g) carrot
3½ oz. (100 g) celery
3½ oz. (100 g) *daikon* sprouts
3½ oz. (100 g) prepared dried *wakame*,
  see page 117
2 oz. (50 g) *harusame*
7 oz. (200 g) squid (body), cleaned and
  skinned
12 small shrimp
1 egg
Dash of salt
A little vegetable oil
NANBANZU DRESSING:
  3 tablespoons miso
  3 tablespoons sugar
  3 tablespoons tomato ketchup
  2 tablespoons shoyu
  1 tablespoon sesame oil
  ⅔ teaspoon *shichimi-togarashi*

1. Slice the *daikon* into 1½" (4 cm) rounds, then cut into julienne strips. **(1)**
2. Cut the carrot and celery into 1½" (4 cm) sticks. Trim the base off the *daikon* sprouts and cut the stems in half.
3. Soak the vegetables in ice water for about 20 minutes or until crisp. Drain.
4. Cut the *wakame* into strips of about ¾" (2 cm). Pour boiling water over it, plunge in cold water and drain well.
5. Soak the *harusame* in lukewarm water for 10 minutes or until soft. Parboil until clear, then rinse and drain. Cut into bite-size pieces.
6. Cut the peeled squid lengthwise into four. Score the surface in a criss-cross fashion and cut into ¾" (2 cm) pieces. Blanch in boiling water, plunge into ice water and drain.   **(2–4)**

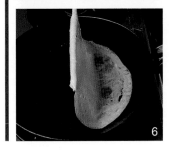

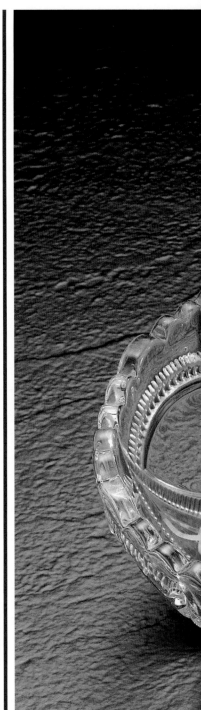

7. Remove the heads of the shrimp and devein. Boil the shrimp until they turn pink. Drain immediately. Once cool, remove the shells.

8. Mix the egg well and add the salt. Pass through a sieve to ensure a smooth texture. Heat a frying pan and wipe the surface with oil. Spread the egg thinly over the surface of the pan and cook, taking care not to burn it. Turn off the heat. Slide a cooking chopstick underneath the egg and lift it out draped over the chopstick. Once slightly cooled, slice it in half. Roll each half up and cut into fine strips. (5–7)

9. Mix the dressing.

10. Combine the vegetables, *waka-me* and *harusame* in a chilled dish. Scatter the squid and shrimp over the top. Serve at the table, allowing guests to help themselves to the dressing.

Squid and Cabbage in Mustard Dressing

Kyabetsu to ika no karashizu

A salad of subtle flavors zipped up with a tangy vinegar and mustard dressing. Blanched cabbage retains a pleasant crunchiness while losing its raw taste.

5 cabbage leaves
  Dash of salt
5 oz. (150 g) squid (body), skinned
  and cleaned
MUSTARD DRESSING:
  3 tablespoons rice vinegar
  3 tablespoons light shoyu
  1 tablespoon sugar
  2 tablespoons dashi stock
  Dash of salt
  ½ tablespoon mustard
GARNISH:
  Bofu (optional)

1. Remove the hard stalk from each cabbage leaf. Slice each leaf lengthwise in half, then crosswise into 1–1½" (3–4 cm) pieces. Layer the pieces and cut into ¾" (2 cm) wide strips. **(1–2)**

2. Blanch the cabbage in boiling salted water, then refresh in cold water. Drain in a colander, then squeeze out the remaining water.

3. Cut the squid lengthwise into four. Bring a pan of water to a rapid boil and dip in each piece of squid, plunging it into ice water immediately afterwards. Wipe dry and cut into thin slices. **(3)**

4. Mix the ingredients for the dressing. Arrange the cabbage and squid in serving bowls and garnish with *bofu*, if using. Pouring on the dressing from above would spoil the appearance of the salad, so add it gently from the side.

Cucumber, *Wakame* and Shrimp in Ginger Dressing

Kyuri, wakame to ebi no shogazu

A refreshing salad that stimulates the appetite, this is ideal as either an appetizer or as a side dish.

2 Japanese cucumbers
3½ oz. (100 g) prepared dried *wakame**
12 small shrimp
 Dash of salt
GINGER DRESSING:
 2 tablespoons rice vinegar
 2 tablespoons light shoyu
 1 tablespoon sugar
 3 tablespoons dashi stock
 1 teaspoon ginger juice, see page 80
GARNISH:
 Bofu (optional)

1. Cut the ends off the cucumbers and slice thinly. Leave to soak in salted water for about 20 minutes or until soft. Squeeze out excess water and refrigerate. **(1–2)**

2. Slice the *wakame* into ¾" (2 cm) pieces. Pour boiling water over it, refresh in cold water and drain well. Refrigerate. **(3)**

3. Remove the heads of the shrimp and devein. Boil for about 1 minute. Let cool in a colander. Once cool, shell the shrimp and refrigerate.

4. Mix the dressing and refrigerate until needed. Just before serving, arrange the cucumber, *wakame* and shrimp in dishes and pour the dressing over the salad. Garnish with *bofu*, if using.

* To prepare dried *wakame*: soak in cold water for 5 minutes before using.

Shoyu-Steeped Spinach
Horenso no ohitashi

Blanched only until vivid green, the spinach absorbs the subtle flavor of the shoyu dressing. The fluffy bonito flakes on top add an interesting flavor to this side dish.

11 oz. (300 g) spinach
  Dash of salt
SHOYU DRESSING:
  1½ tablespoons light shoyu
  ¾ cup dashi stock
GARNISH:
  Bonito flakes

1. Trim off the spinach roots. Cut a cross ½" (1 cm) deep into the base of any thick stems. Wash well and drain.
2. Bring a pot of water to a boil. Salt it and add the spinach, stems first. Cook for just 10 seconds, then remove.
3. Plunge the spinach immediately into cold water changed two or three times or hold it under cold running water. Holding the stems under water, squeeze out the excess water.   **(1–2)**
4. Mix the shoyu and dashi in a long shallow dish. Lay the spinach in the dressing and refrigerate for about 30 minutes.   **(3)**
5. Keeping the spinach lengths tightly together, squeeze out any excess liquid and cut into 1½" (4 cm) lengths. Place the small bundles in serving bowls and pour over a little of the shoyu mixture. Sprinkle generously with bonito flakes.

* For a colorful variation, add yellow chrysanthemum petals. Pick the petals of 5–6 large flowers and blanch in boiling water. Squeeze out excess water and leave to cool. Soak in the shoyu mixture and mix with the spinach.

String Beans in Sesame Dressing

Sayaingen no goma-ae

Crunchy string beans are mixed with a fragrant dressing made from ground toasted sesame seeds. Substitute seasonal vegetables or mushrooms to adapt the dish to the season.

7 oz. (200 g) string beans
  Dash of salt
1 teaspoon light shoyu
SESAME DRESSING:
  4 tablespoons toasted sesame seeds
  1 tablespoon saké
  1 tablespoon sugar
  ½ tablespoon shoyu
  Dash of salt

1. Cook the beans for 2–3 minutes in salted boiling water. Drain in a colander and leave to cool. **(1)**
2. Top and tail the beans and cut into 1" (3 cm) lengths. Season with a little shoyu. **(2)**
3. Grind the sesame using a pestle and mortar or blend in a food processor. Add the saké, sugar, shoyu and salt and blend. **(3)**
4. Just before serving, mix the beans with the sesame dressing.

Stir-Fried *Kimpira*
Kimpira san-shu

Crunchy strips of vegetable are stir-fried only until the spicy seasonings are absorbed. Burdock is the best known form of *kimpira*, but the recipe can be adapted to suit other vegetables too.

Burdock *Kimpira*
Gobo no kimpira

3½ oz. (100 g) burdock
1 oz. (30 g) carrot
1½ tablespoons vegetable oil
SEASONINGS:
  1 tablespoon saké
  1 tablespoon mirin
  1½ tablespoons sugar
  1½ tablespoons shoyu
  ½ teaspoon *shichimi-togarashi*

1. Scrub the burdock with a brush under running water. Closely score the length of the burdock with a knife. As if sharpening a pencil, shave off 1½" (4 cm) lengths of burdock. Leave to soak in cold water. **(1–2)**
2. After 10 minutes, transfer to a colander. Rinse quickly and drain.
3. Cut the carrot into julienne strips about 1½" (4 cm) long.
4. Heat the oil in a frying pan and stir-fry the burdock. Add the carrot and cook over a high heat until both the burdock and the carrot are evenly coated with the oil. Over medium heat add the seasonings and cook until all the liquid has been absorbed. Place in a shallow serving dish and sprinkle with *shichimi-togarashi*. **(3–6)**

Lotus Root *Kimpira*
Renkon no kimpira

3½ oz. (100 g) lotus root
1 tablespoon vegetable oil
SEASONINGS:
  2 tablespoons mirin
  1 tablespoon light shoyu
  1 small red chilli pepper, chopped finely

1. Peel a thick layer of skin off the lotus root. Slice the root and cut each slice in half. Soak for 3–4 minutes in water to get rid of any bitterness. Rinse and drain well.
2. Heat the oil in a frying pan and stir-fry the lotus root over high heat. Add the seasonings and continue to cook until the seasonings are completely absorbed. Transfer to a serving dish.

Celery *Kimpira*
Serori no kimpira

3½ oz. (100 g) celery
1 tablespoon vegetable oil
1 small red chilli pepper, chopped finely
SEASONINGS:
  1 tablespoon saké
  1 tablespoon light shoyu
  Dash of salt

1. Remove any tough fibers from the celery and cut into thin sticks about 1½" (4 cm) long.
2. Heat the oil in a frying pan and stir-fry the celery and chilli pepper. Add the seasonings and mix. Tilt the pan to reduce the sauce while keeping the celery away from the heat to prevent further cooking. Mix and transfer to a serving dish.

Two-Tone Eggplant
Bei-nasu no ni-shoku dengaku

A dish spread liberally with miso paste is called a *dengaku*. This recipe uses two different colors of miso paste for a stunning effect.

2 large eggplants
Vegetable oil for deep-frying
WHITE MISO SPREAD:
  ½ cup white miso
  1 tablespoon sugar
  ½ cup mirin
RED MISO SPREAD:
  ½ cup red miso
  2 tablespoons sugar
  ½ cup mirin
CUCUMBER RINGS:
  ½ Japanese cucumber
  3 tablespoons rice vinegar
  3 tablespoons dashi stock
  Dash of salt
GARNISH:
  White poppy seeds

1. Using a corer, hollow out the center of the cucumber and discard. Slice the cucumber thinly. Dip in boiling water and plunge into cold water immediately. Mix the vinegar, dashi and salt. Drain the cucumber and leave to soak in this mixture.
2. Mix the white miso and sugar in a pan. Add the mirin a little at a time. Stir over low heat for about 20 minutes to thicken the mixture, taking care not to burn it. Once the mixture has thickened, remove from heat. Make the red miso spread in the same way. **(1–3)**
3. Trim the stem of the eggplant, leaving a little for decorative effect. Cut the eggplants lengthwise in half and score the flesh diagonally in a criss-cross fashion to make it easy to eat with chopsticks. Slice off a small piece of skin from the underside of each half to create a stable base. **(4–5)**
4. Heat the oil to about 340°F (170°C). Lower the eggplants into the oil, skin side down. After 2–3 minutes, reduce

the heat slightly and turn over. Cook
for a further 2–3 minutes. **(6–7)**
5. Drain well and spread with the miso
pastes. Sprinkle with poppy seeds and
garnish with cucumber rings.

Summer Vegetables
Natsu yasai no takiawase

To bring out the subtle flavors of this dish, each ingredient is cooked separately. The end result makes the extra effort worthwhile.

1 lb. (500 g) Japanese squash
SQUASH BOILING BROTH:
  3 cups dashi stock
  2 tablespoons saké
  2 tablespoons mirin
  3 tablespoons sugar
  1 tablespoon light shoyu
  ⅕ teaspoon salt
8 small eggplants (or 2 regular eggplants)
Vegetable oil for deep-frying
EGGPLANT BOILING BROTH:
  2 cups dashi stock
  1 tablespoon saké
  1 tablespoon mirin
  1½ tablespoons sugar
  2 tablespoons shoyu
  ⅕ teaspoon salt
8 oz. (250g) raw *yuba*
YUBA BOILING BROTH:
  2 cups dashi stock
  1 tablespoon saké
  2 tablespoons sugar
  2 tablespoons mirin
  2 tablespoons light shoyu
  ⅕ teaspoon salt
24 stalks *mitsuba*
5 large shrimp
3½ oz. (100g) string beans
  Dash of salt
BEAN BOILING BROTH:
  1½ cups dashi stock
  1 tablespoon saké
  2 tablespoons light shoyu
  ⅕ teaspoon salt
GARNISH:
  Green *yuzu* peel

1. Scoop out the pulp and seeds from the squash. Peel roughly, leaving some skin on, and cut into 1½" (3–4 cm) cubes. Soak briefly in cold water, then drain. **(1–2)**

2. Place the squash and its boiling broth in a pan. Cover with a drop lid or paper and cook over a medium heat until soft. Remove from heat and let stand to allow the squash to absorb the flavors.

3. Peel the eggplants and trim the stems. Keeping the eggplants intact, make a series of fine vertical cuts (see Tea Whisk Eggplant, page 19) from the base upwards. Deep-fry in hot oil (about 340°F, 170°C) for 3–4 minutes, then drain. Holding the stem, press down on each eggplant to flatten the base. Place the eggplants in a colander and rinse off excess oil with boiling water. **(3–4)**

4. Bring the broth for the eggplants to a boil and add the eggplants. Cover and cook over medium heat for 5 minutes. Remove from heat and let stand.

5. Cut the *yuba* into 3½" (9 cm) squares. Pile up the squares and cut in half. Tie up the bundles with thread.

6. Bring the broth for the *yuba* to a boil. Add the *yuba* bundles and cook over a low heat for 4–5 minutes. Remove from heat and let stand. **(5–6)**

7. Devein the shrimp and thread each vertically onto a bamboo skewer to prevent them from curling up during cooking. Boil in salted water until they just turn pink. Remove the shells and skewers, leaving the tails intact. **(7–8)**

8. String the beans and cut in half. Bring the broth for them to the boil and add the beans. Cook only until crunchy. Remove the pan from the heat and rest in a basin of ice water.

9. Remove the thread from the *yuba* and cut both bundles into 6 pieces. Tie each with blanched *mitsuba* stems. Drain the other ingredients and arrange carefully in dishes. Sprinkle with *yuzu*.

* To served chilled, refrigerate each ingredient in its own broth. Arrange just before serving.

* To serve hot, briefly reheat each ingredient in its broth.

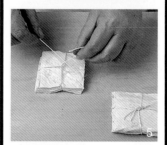

Quick Pickles
Yasai no momi-zuke ni-shu

These instant pickles are really midway between salads and pickles: fresh and crunchy yet with the concentrated flavor only pickles have. They are doubly delicious served straight from the refrigerator.

Pickled Cabbage
Kyabetsu no momi-zuke

Just over 1 lb. (500 g) cabbage
1½ oz. (40 g) carrots
7 oz. (200 g) Japanese cucumbers
20 green *shiso* leaves
1 tablespoon salt

1. Cut out the hard stalk of the cabbage and layer the leaves. Slice lengthwise into ¾" (2 cm), then crosswise into 1½" (4 cm) lengths.
2. Cut the carrots into thin strips ⅕" x 1" (5 mm x 3 cm). Slice the cucumber thinly. Cut the green *shiso* leaves lengthwise in half. Roll them up and slice finely. **(1)**
3. Put the sliced vegetables in a large bowl and sprinkle with salt. Mix and knead with your hands, gently at first but gradually applying more and more pressure. Once the vegetables begin to wilt, squeeze out as much water as possible and place in a serving dish. **(2–3)**

Pickled White Turnips
Kokabu no momi-zuke

5 small white turnips, about 11 oz. (330 g)
3 oz. (80 g) turnip greens
1½ teaspoons salt
Juice and peel of ½ lemon

1. Peel the turnips and slice thinly. Dip the turnip greens in boiling salted water and plunge into cold water. Squeeze out the excess water and cut into ¾" (2 cm) lengths.　　**(1–2)**

2. Put the turnips and the turnip greens in a bowl and sprinkle with the salt. Knead well, gradually exerting more pressure. When they begin to wilt, squeeze out as much water as possible. Refrigerate until needed. Just before serving, sprinkle with lemon juice and slivers of lemon peel.　　**(3–5)**

Fluffy Steamed Rice
Gohan

The key to plump fluffy rice is to soak the rice before cooking. This allows it to absorb enough water to stay moist.

To wash the rice:
1. Put the rice in a pot and cover with water. Swirl your hand twice around the pot in a large circular motion. Replace the water and repeat once or twice. This gets rid of any impurities in the rice. **(1–3)**
2. Squeeze the grains of rice together, changing the water 4 or 5 times, or until it is no longer cloudy.
3. Transfer the washed rice to a colander and drain. **(4)**

To cook the rice:
1. Put the rice in a heavy pan and pour 3¼cups water to every 3 cups rice over it. Let stand for 1–3 hours. **(5)**
2. Cover with a lid and cook over high heat. After the water has been boiling for 30 seconds, turn the heat down to very low and continue to cook for 14–15 minutes. Briefly turn up the heat again, then remove from heat.
3. Without removing the lid, leave the rice to steam for about 10 minutes. Using a wet wooden rice paddle, pull the rice away from the sides of the pot and gently fluff it up.

* This proportion is for most rice. Increase this to just over 3½ cups for old rice, but use only 3 cups for new rice.

Harvest Rice

Aki no takikomi-gohan

Walnuts and assorted mushrooms give this dish a rich autumnal flavor. If you have the time, try your hand at the colorful garnish of fallen leaves—it is easier than it looks!

3 cups rice
3¼ cups water
5 fresh *shiitake* mushrooms
3½ oz. (100 g) *shimeji* mushrooms
3½ oz. (100 g) *enoki* mushrooms
10 shelled walnuts
1 sheet *aburage*
SEASONINGS:
  3 tablespoons saké
  3 tablespoons shoyu
  ½ teaspoon salt
  ½ teaspoon sugar
GARNISHES:
  Cooked leaf-shaped carrots,
  kamaboko, egg , burdock and
  gingko nuts

Maple and gingko leaf-shaped
  cutters*

1. Wash and soak the rice at least one hour before cooking. Place in a pot with 3½ cups water.
2. Wipe the *shiitake* mushrooms with a damp cloth and remove the stems. Cut into quarters.
3. Rinse the *shimeji* mushrooms quickly and break into clumps of 2–3 mushrooms. Cut off the base of the *enoki*. Quickly rinse and loosen the stalks.
4. Chop each walnut roughly into 2–3 pieces. Rinse the *aburage* with boiling water to get rid of excess oil. Cut lengthwise in halves, then crosswise into thin strips. **(1)**
5. Put the mushrooms and walnuts into a saucepan and add the seasonings. Mix roughly with a rice paddle. Cover and cook over high heat. **(2–3)**
6. Turn the heat down to very low 30 seconds after the rice comes to a boil and cook for 15 minutes. Turn up the

heat briefly, then remove from heat. Let stand for 10 minutes to steam.

7. Fluff up the rice with a rice paddle and cover again for 10 seconds. Serve onto plates and scatter the "leaves" over the top.   (4–5)

* If leaf-shaped cutters are not available, any small cutters would do. Otherwise, try the decorative cuts on page 19.

For the Carrot Maple Leaves:

Slice a carrot into ⅕" (5 mm) slices and use a maple leaf cutter to cut out leaf shapes. Cook for 5 minutes in a stock of 4 tablespoons dashi, 1 tablespoon sugar and a dash of salt. Set aside for the carrot to absorb the flavors.

For the *Kamaboko* Gingko Leaves:

Cut 20 slices of ⅕" (5 mm) thick *kamaboko* using a gingko-shaped cutter. Heat a metal skewer and make scorch marks on each "leaf."

For the Egg Gingko Leaves:

Mix an egg with a dash of salt and a little *katakuriko* dissolved in water. Spread thinly over the surface of a hot frying pan and cook. Cut out leaves using a gingko-shaped cutter.

For the Burdock Pine Needles:

Cut two 1½" (4 cm) lengths of burdock into thin strips. Cut each strip lengthwise but leave it intact at one end. Cook in a stock of 3 tablespoons dashi and 1 tablespoon each of saké and shoyu until the stock is completely absorbed.

For the Gingko Nuts:

Shell and boil the nuts. Roast them in a dry frying pan and sprinkle with ⅓ teaspoon salt and 1 tablespoon saké.

Harvest Rice➡

Savory Rice Balls
Onigiri san-shu

The Japanese equivalent to a sandwich, rice balls (*onigiri*) can be barrel-shaped, triangular or round, plain or toasted, and filled with anything you care to name. They are a good way to use up leftover cooked rice, and as finger food, they are ideal for packed lunches.

6–10 cups cooked rice made from
  3 cups of uncooked rice
3–4 *umeboshi* or substitute fillings
  (salt-broiled and flaked salmon, shoyu-steeped bonito flakes, canned tuna, red caviar, etc.)
4 sheets *nori*, 2″ x 5″ (5 cm x 12 cm)
Salt to taste
Vegetable oil as needed
Shoyu to taste

1. Stone the *umeboshi* and tear the flesh into 12 pieces of about ½″ (1.5 cm).
2. Place a small handful of rice for one rice ball in a rice bowl (or any small round bowl). Use slightly more for a barrel-shaped rice ball than for the round or triangular ones. Make a small well in the center of the rice and place a piece of *umeboshi* inside. Shake the bowl gently to form the rice into a rough ball. Repeat for each of the three kinds of rice balls. Wet your hands and sprinkle with a little salt before shaping to prevent the rice from sticking too much.   **(1–2)**

3. To make rice barrels, cup one hand to hold the rice. Cupping your other hand, press both ends of the barrel while turning and rolling it into shape. Gradually increase the pressure. Wrap a piece of *nori* around each barrel.   **(3)**

4. Make round rice balls by placing the rice in one hand and rolling it into a ball with your other hand.
5. Make triangular rice balls by using one cupped hand to form the base of the triangle. Bending your other hand at the knuckles, press the rice to form the other two sides of the triangle. Turn

and repeat until it forms a regular triangle. Heat a frying pan and wipe the surface with a little oil. Lay the rice balls in the pan and cook until browned. Remove from heat and brush with shoyu. Return to the heat to the outside. Repeat two or three times for each side.   **(4–5)**

Green Pea Rice

Ao-mame gohan

The color and fragrance of fresh green peas make this dish a favorite among the Japanese in early summer. A delicious but simple way to appreciate this seasonal vegetable.

3 cups rice
1 cup freshly shelled green peas
SEASONINGS:
  3 tablespoons saké
  1 teaspoon salt
  1 teaspoon light shoyu

1. Wash and soak the rice at least one hour prior to cooking. Place in a pot with 2½ cups of water.
2. Soak the peas for 5 minutes in 2 cups of water mixed with 1 teaspoon of salt. Drain, reserving the water.
3. Bring this water to a boil and add the green peas. After 4–5 minutes remove from heat. When they have cooled, drain the peas, again reserving the water. **(1–2)**
4. Add 1 cup of this water and the seasonings to the rice. Cover and cook over high heat. Reduce the heat to very low 30–40 seconds after the rice comes to a boil and cook for 14–15 minutes. Add the green peas, turn up the heat briefly and remove from heat. **(3–4)**
5. Leave covered to steam for 10 minutes. Transfer to a serving dish or a *handai* (as shown in the photograph) and fluff up the rice before serving.

Shrimp Tempura Bowl
Ten-don

A delicious combination of crispy shrimp tempura dipped in a light sauce and arranged on a bowl of steaming hot rice.

4–6 cups cooked rice made from
  2 cups uncooked rice
20 shrimp
8 *shishi-togarashi* peppers
Flour for coating
Vegetable oil for deep-frying
BATTER:
  1 lightly beaten egg topped up
    to 1 cup with cold water
  1 cup all-purpose flour
DIPPING SAUCE:
  ½ cup mirin
  ¼ cup shoyu
  1 tablespoon sugar
  2 tablespoons dashi stock

1. Shell and devein the shrimp. Mix the batter lightly, leaving it lumpy. Dip the shrimp first in flour, then in the batter. Deep-fry five at a time and drain. Coat and deep-fry the *shishi-togarashi* in the same way. **(1)**

2. Bring the ingredients for the sauce to a boil. Divide the rice between four deep bowls and pour 1½ tablespoons of sauce over each. **(2)**

3. Dip the shrimp in the remaining sauce and arrange on the rice, tails pointing inward. Repeat with the *shishi-togarashi* and place in front of the shrimp. Cover with a lid, if available, and serve immediately. **(3)**

135

Hand-Wrapped Sushi

Temaki-zushi

Prepare a large platter of attractively arranged meat, fish, vegetables, *nori*, rolled egg, and, of course, *sushi* rice. Guests wrap their own choice of fillings in a sheet of *nori.* Great fun for parties.

SUSHI RICE:
  2 cups uncooked rice
  1 sheet *kombu*, 2" x 2" (5 cm x 5 cm)
  ¼ cup Japanese rice vinegar
  ½ tablespoon sugar
  ½ tablespoon salt
FILLINGS:
  10 sheets *nori*, 8" x 8" (20 cm x 20 cm)
  10 green *shiso* leaves
  3½ oz. (100 g) *daikon* sprouts
  8–10 stalks *asatsuki* or 3 green onions
  3½ oz. (100 g) corned beef or ham
  7 oz. (200 g) raw tuna fillet
  Rolled eggs made from 5 eggs (see
    pages 66–68) shaped into a block
  1 avocado
  Dash of lemon juice
CONDIMENTS:
  2–3 teaspoons *wasabi* paste
  2–3 tablespoons shoyu

1. Wash and soak the rice in 2¼ cups of water at least one hour before cooking.
2. Add the *kombu* and place over high heat. Remove the *kombu* once the water comes to a boil. Cook the rice over low heat for 13–14 minutes. Turn up the heat briefly, then remove from heat. Let stand for 8 minutes. **(1–2)**
3. Mix the vinegar with the sugar and salt. Dip the rice paddle in the vinegar mixture and use it to transfer the steamed rice to a *handai* or large shallow dish. Pour the vinegar mixture over the rice a little at a time and, with the paddle, mix in the vinegar swiftly but gently. Fanning the rice at the same time gives a better flavor.* **(3–5)**
4. Lightly toast the *nori* and cut each sheet into quarters. Wash the *daikon* sprouts and remove the base. Cut the

asatsuki into 2″ (5 cm) lengths.

5. Cut the corned beef, tuna and egg into sticks of ½″ x 2″ (1 cm x 5 cm).

6. Cut around the avocado lengthwise. Twist and open. Peel off the skin and remove the stone. Mash the flesh with the lemon juice.

7. Arrange all the ingredients except for the *nori* and shoyu on a large serving platter. The *wasabi* adds a piquancy to the tuna and avocado, so place a mound of it near these two ingredients. Serve the *nori* and shoyu in separate dishes. Guests help themselves to a sheet of *nori* and roll rice and fillings up inside. **(6–7)**

* A fan to cool the rice. If a fan is not abailable, a piece of stiff card can also be used.

Sushi Balls

Temari-zushi

Like Christmas baubles, these bite-sized balls are bright and colorful. A different seasoning for each fish adds to the variety of flavors.

Makes 30 balls:
2 oz. (50 g) tuna fillet
2 oz. (50 g) sea bream
2 oz. (50 g) squid (body), cleaned and peeled
1 whole *sayori* (halfbeak)*
½ tablespoon Japanese rice vinegar
3 thin slices smoked salmon
6 sprigs *kinome*
SUSHI RICE:
  2 cups uncooked rice
  1 sheet of *kombu,* 2" x 2"
    (5 cm x 5 cm)
  ¼ cup Japanese rice vinegar
  ½ tablespoon sugar
  ½ tablespoon salt
GARNISHES:
  6 *mi-zansho tsukudani* seeds or capers
  Wasabi and mustard
  A little mashed *umeboshi*
2–3 tablespoons shoyu to serve

1. Prepare sushi rice as for Hand-Wrapped Sushi (see page 136).
2. Holding the knife at an angle, slice the tuna thinly into squares of about 1½" (3.5 cm). Slice the sea bream and the peeled squid in the same way. Cut the smoked salmon into squares the same size.
3. Fillet the *sayori* and rub vinegar into the skin. Peel off the thin skin from the head towards the tail. Cut into squares of ½" (3.5 cm). **(1–4)**
4. Divide the rice into 30 portions. Lay a portion of rice on a piece of saran wrap and twist the corners together, so that the rice forms a rough ball shape. **(5)**
5. Lay a slice of tuna on a damp cloth and place the rice ball on top. Twist the cloth together to form a sphere. Press the top of each ball to set the fish in place. Repeat with the remaining rice and fish.

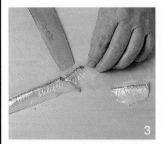

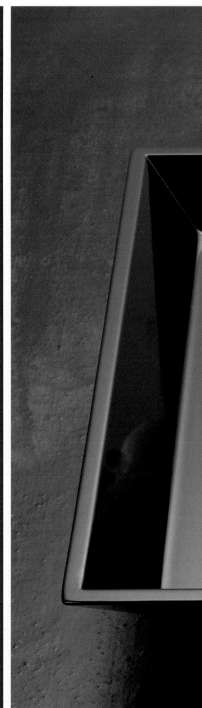

When preparing the sea bream balls, sandwich a sprig of *kinome* between the fish and the rice. (6–7)
6. Garnish the tuna balls with a dot of mustard, the squid balls with a dot of *wasabi*, the smoked salmon with *mizansho* and the *sayori* with *wasabi* and mashed *umeboshi*. Arrange the sushi balls decoratively on a serving dish and serve with small dishes of shoyu. Dip the balls in shoyu before eating.

* *Sayori* (halfbeak)is a slender fish with white flesh. It has a light and delicate taste. If unavailable, an uncooked ham (Parma, Bayonne, Westphalian, etc.) makes a good substitute.

Foxy Noodles

Kitsune udon

These *udon* noodles are served in a light broth and topped with sweet *aburage* and finely chopped scallions. The unusual name of the dish stems from a traditional belief that the fox, messenger to the god Inari, was partial to *aburage*.

1 lb. (400–500 g) dried *udon* noodles
BROTH:
   6 cups water
   1½ oz. (40 g) bonito flakes
   1½ tablespoons saké
   1½ tablespoons light shoyu
   2 teaspoons salt
ABURAGE COOKING BROTH:
   2 sheets *aburage*
   1 cup dashi stock
   2 tablespoons sugar
   1 tablespoon saké
   1 tablespoon mirin
   1 tablespoon light shoyu
GARNISH:
   ½ white part of *negi*, cut into 2″
     (5 cm) lengths
   Shichimi-togarashi or powdered *sansho*

1. Bring the ingredients for the broth to a boil. Reduce the heat and skim off any scum. Cook for 2–3 minutes over low heat. Pour through a very fine sieve or one lined with a clean cloth.
2. Rinse the *aburage* with boiling water to get rid of excess oil. Cut each sheet into 4–6 triangles. **(1)**
3. Bring the dashi to a boil and add the sugar and saké. Cook the *aburage* in the stock for 2–3 minutes. Add the mirin and light shoyu and cover with a drop lid or aluminum foil. Continue to cook until all the stock is absorbed. **(2)**
4. Bring a large pot of water to a boil. Add the noodles and stir to prevent them from sticking together. When the water is on the point of boiling over, add ½ cup cold water. Repeat this process, adding more water only when the water is nearly boiling over. Boil

until a little softer than *al dente*. (3–5)
5. Place the noodles in a colander and set in a bowl. Pour over cold water and rinse. Change the water a few times until the water runs clear and drain.
6. To serve, soak the *udon* briefly in boiling water. Drain and divide between serving bowls. Add *negi* and

ladle over the hot soup. Arrange with triangles of the *aburage* on top. Garnish with shredded *negi* and sprinkle with *shichimi-togarashi* or powdered *sansho*, if desired. (6–8)

Nanban Duck and Noodles
Kamo nanban

Literally, *nanban* means "southern bar-barian"; it was used to refer to the for-eigners who came to Japan in the six-teenth century. Nowadays, however, the term refers merely to dishes which include non-traditional ingredients. It is the leek and chilli pepper which give this rich noodle dish its name.

1 lb. (400–500 g) dried *udon* noodles
BROTH:
  6 cups water
  1½ oz. (40 g) bonito flakes
  4 tablespoons saké
  4½ tablespoons sugar
  4½ tablespoons mirin
  ¾ cup shoyu
  ¼ teaspoon salt
11–14 oz. (300–400 g) duck meat
2–3 leeks, cut into 1" (3 cm) lengths
1½ tablespoons vegetable oil

Shichimi-togarashi or powdered *sansho*
  to serve

1. Prepare the broth and *udon* noodles (see page 140).
2. Trim away the fat off the duck. Cut the meat into thin slices.   **(1)**
3. Heat a frying pan and wipe with the oil. Add the leeks and brown over high heat. Add the duck and brown both sides quickly.   **(2)**
4. Bring the soup to a boil and add the duck and leeks. Reheat the noodles and place in serving bowls. Ladle over the soup, duck and leeks. Sprinkle with *shichimi-togarashi* or powdered *sansho*, if desired.   **(3)**

Swirled Egg Noodles
Tamago-toji udon

This mild dish of green vegetables in a lightly cooked egg topping over *udon* noodles is good for weight-watchers and for the occasional midnight snack.

1 lb. (400–500 g) dried *udon* noodles
BROTH:
  6 cups dashi stock
  1 tablespoon saké
  3 tablespoons sugar
  2 tablespoons mirin
  4 tablespoons light shoyu
  ¼ teaspoon salt
TOPPING:
  4 eggs
  3½ oz. (100 g) *mitsuba* or cooked
    spinach
Shichimi-togarashi or powdered *sansho*
  to serve

1. Bring the dashi to a boil and add the other seasonings. As soon as the soup returns to a boil, remove from heat.
2. As each serving is cooked individually, break the eggs into four separate dishes and stir gently. Cut the *mitsuba* into 1½" (4 cm) lengths.
3. Cook the *udon* noodles (see page 120) and rinse. To reheat, soak briefly in boiling water, drain and divide between four bowls.
4. Bring ¼ of the soup mixture to the boil. Scatter with ¼ of the *mitsuba* and pour over one of the eggs. As soon as the egg becomes half-set and fluffy, slide the mixture over one serving of noodles. Repeat for the other three servings. Sprinkle with *shichimi-togarashi* or powdered *sansho*, if desired.   **(1–2)**

Desserts

Fruit Salad with Silky Rice Drops
Furutsu Shiratama

Jazz up summer fruit salads with these red and white silky-smooth drops. Simple to make, they are the colors traditionally associated with happiness and good fortune. Delicious served chilled on hot summer days.

WHITE RICE DROPS:
  ⅓ cup *shiratamako*
  2 tablespoons water
RED RICE DROPS:
  ⅓ cup *shiratamako*
  2 tablespoons water
  Dash of red food coloring
FRUIT:
  8–12 dried prunes, stoned
  Black tea for soaking the prunes
  4 canned apricots
  8–12 canned mandarin segments
  1–2 kiwi fruit
SYRUP:
  ½ cup sugar
  ¼ cup water
  Juice of one lemon
  3–4 tablespoons of syrup from the
    canned fruit
  1–2 tablespoons honey

1. Make some black tea and pour just enough over the prunes to cover them. Leave to cool, then refrigerate until needed. **(1)**
2. Dissolve the sugar in hot water and leave to cool. Add the lemon juice, syrup and honey to taste. Refrigerate until needed.
3. Cut each apricot into 3–4 pieces. Peel the kiwi fruit and cut either into round slices or half-rounds. Mix with the mandarins and refrigerate.
4. Put the *shiratamako* for the white drops in a bowl and add water, a little at a time. Mix until smooth. Divide into pieces the size of the top half of your thumb. Do the same for the red rice drops. **(2–6)**
5. Bring a large pan of water to a boil

over medium heat. Roll the pieces into balls, using your middle finger and thumb to make an indentation in the center of each. Drop the balls in the boiling water a few at a time, scooping them out as soon as they float to the surface. Soak the cooked drops in cold water. (7)

6. To serve, arrange the drained prunes and other fruits in chilled bowls. Drain the rice drops and scatter over the fruit. Drizzle the syrup over the top.

* Another exotic addition to a fruit salad is *nata-de-coco*, as shown in the photograph. Made from coconuts, it has a firm jelly-like texture.

Sweet Potato Candy

Satsuma-imo no chakin shibori

A major attraction of Japanese candies and desserts is that they are almost all fat-free! This candy is both healthy and simple to make. Twisting the mixture in a cloth gives the candy its unusual shape, while *matcha* green tea powder provides the subtle pattern.

11 oz. (300 g) sweet potatoes
1 *kuchinashi-no-mi* (gardenia fruit),
  if available
5–6 tablespoons sugar
Dash of salt
1 teaspoon *matcha* powder
  or green food coloring

1. Break the *kuchinashi-no-mi* in half, if using. Wrap in gauze and soak in one cup of cold water.
2. Peel a thick layer of skin off the sweet potato and cut into ¾" (2 cm) slices. Soak immediately in cold water to prevent discoloration.   **(1)**
3. Drain and place in a pan with just enough water to cover the sweet potato. If using, add the *kuchinashi-no-mi* and its water to color the sweet potato as it cooks. Boil until soft and drain in a colander.   **(2)**
4. Mash or strain the sweet potato while it is still hot. Add the salt and sugar and cook over low heat for 2–3 minutes, stirring with a wooden spoon. Leave to cool.   **(3–4)**
5. Add just under a teaspoon of boiling water to the *matcha* powder. Mix until smooth.
6. Blend approximately 2 tablespoons of the sweet potato mixture with the *matcha* paste.   **(5)**
7. Soak a piece of fine gauze or a clean cloth in water and wring out well. Lay ⅙ of the yellow mixture inside, spreading it out a little with your palms. Add ⅙ of the green mixture at one corner. Pick up the the gauze pack by its four corners and hold it in one cupped hand. Twist the corners of the gauze

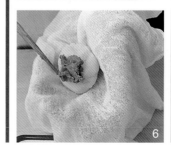

together using your other hand and
unwrap. Form the other candies in the
same way.   (6–8)

* You can make the candies smaller if you
prefer and use any leftover mixture to make
small balls on skewers.

Adzuki Bean Dessert
Zenzai

Red adzuki beans boiled until soft and sweetened with sugar make a healthy dessert. Add silky rice drops (see page 124) or *mochi* rice cakes for a mid-afternoon snack.

2 cups adzuki beans (11oz., 300 g)
3 cups sugar
½ teaspoon salt

1. Place the adzuki beans in a bowl under running water. Swirl your hand through the beans to wash them, discarding imperfect ones. Drain.　**(1)**
2. Bring the beans and 6 cups of water to a boil over high heat. When they begin to boil, add another ½ cup of water and continue to cook over high heat. When the pot returns to a boil, add another ½ cup of water. Repeat once or twice.　**(2–3)**
3. Skim scum off the surface and cook for 40–60 minutes or until tender. Test the beans by crushing one between your thumb and little finger.　**(4)**
4. Add the sugar and cook over medium heat for 7–8 minutes. Add the salt and remove from heat. Serve either hot or cold, but as it is sweet, serve small helpings only.　**(5–6)**

* This dessert can be served as soon as it is cooked, but letting it stand overnight gives it a thicker consistency and richer taste. It can keep as long as a week in an airtight container in the refrigerator because of its high sugar content.

Adzuki Bean Jelly
Mizu-yokan

A smooth dessert made from pureed adzuki beans (*neri-an*) set in an agar agar solution. Its sweetness goes very well with the slight bitterness of green tea.

Makes enough for a 5½″ x 6½″ (16 cm x 14 cm) tray:
1 stick agar agar (⅓ oz., 10 g)
3 cups water
3–3½ oz. (90–100 g) sugar
14 oz. (400 g) can *neri-an* (sweetened)
⅕ teaspoon salt

1. Rinse the agar agar and tear into four pieces. Cover with water and soak for 30 minutes or until soft. To prevent the agar agar from floating up, rest a light plate directly on top of it. **(1)**
2. Wrap the agar agar in a cloth and squeeze out the excess water. Tear into fine pieces and place in a pan. Add the water and cook over medium heat, stirring until it has dissolved. **(2)**
3. Strain through a sieve into another pan. Add the sugar and stir over medium heat until dissolved. Remove from heat and add the *neri-an.* **(3–4)**
4. Return to the heat and add the salt. When the mixture comes to a boil, lower the heat and simmer for 3–4 minutes, stirring constantly. Stand the pan in a basin of ice water and stir the mixture to reduce its temperature.
5. Rinse the tray in cold water, as the water will help the jelly slide out once set. Stand the tray in a basin of ice water and pour in the bean mixture. Refrigerate until set. **(5)**
6. Turn out of the tray and cut into eight pieces using a wet knife. Alternatively, cut the jelly in the tray, resting a chopstick over the tray as a guide.

* If using homemade *neri-an* (see Glossary), omit the sugar and salt.

Glossary * See color plates, pages 10–14.

Aburage (Tofu Puff)*
Aburage is tofu which has been deep-fried until golden and puffy. Unlike other kinds of tofu, *aburage* is not stored under water. For the recipes in this book, buy the thin sheets of *aburage*, not the blocks. Rinse off the excess oil with boiling water before using.
   To store: Wrapped in plastic and refrigerated, *aburage* will last for 5–7 days.
   See also Tofu.

Adzuki Beans*
These small red beans are widely available in the West, but are generally not used to make sweet dishes as they are in the East. Pureed adzuki beans (*an*) is a basic ingredient to many Japanese candies and desserts. It can be bought ready-made or prepared at home.
   See Neri-an.

Agar-agar (Kanten)*
A gelling agent made from seaweed used in Japanese confectionery. Available in stick, thread and powdered forms, its texture is more brittle and delicate than that of gelatin.
   Substitute: Gelatin can be used but produces a different texture.

Aonoriko
This powdered green seaweed is used as a condiment, as in Green-Fried Chicken.
   To store: Keep in an airtight container.

Asatsuki*
Asatsuki is the slimmest member of the leek family. Its green stems are finely chopped and used as a garnish for their strong and pungent flavor.
   Substitute: Scallions or chives.
   See also Wakegi.

Atari-goma
This sesame paste can be bought ready-made or made at home. To make, grind toasted white sesame seeds in a pestle and mortar until creamy and then strain. Ready-made *atari-goma* is also available.

Baby Cucumbers (Morokyu)*
Baby cucumbers are used as garnishes for chilled summer dishes.
   Substitute: Peeled and de-seeded Western cucumber.
   See also Baby Cucumbers with Flowers

Baby Cucumbers with Flowers (Hana-tsuki-kyuri)*
Used as a garnish for chilled summer dishes, these gherkins are fresh and unpickled. The combination of the green gherkin with its yellow flowers makes a stunning garnish.
   Substitute: Any small edible green leaves.

Beni-tade*
Consisting of tiny reddish-purple leaves and stems, *beni-tade* is used as a garnish, especially for white fish sashimi. It has a slightly peppery flavor but is used primarily for its color.
   Substitute: For an alternative red garnish, try finely sliced radish or raddichio leaves.

Bofu*
A member of the dropwort family, *bofu* has a distinctive aroma. It is widely used as a garnish for sashimi, soup and cooked fish dishes. It has small but thick green leaves and a dark red stem.

Bonito Flakes (Kezuri-bushi)
An essential in any Japanese kitchen, bonito flakes are one of the two ingredients for dashi stock. They are also used as a condiment and

garnish, as for instance in Shoyu-Steeped Spinach or Deep-Fried Tofu. Every home used to shave flakes from a block of dried bonito on a daily basis, but nowadays most Japanese rely on the packaged variety.
   To choose: Look for the lightest color flakes.
   To store: Refrigerate in an airtight container. After opening, they will last for up to 3 weeks.

Burdock (Gobo)*
This long brown stem has a fairly neutral flavor but is used in such dishes as Kimpira for its pleasant crunchiness and ability to absorb other flavors.
   To store: Wrapped in plastic and refrigerated it can last up to 2 weeks.

Cloud Ear Mushrooms (Kikurage)
This edible fungus is used more for its soft but crunchy texture and dark color than for its neutral flavor. The translation of the Japanese name is "tree jellyfish," but in English it is known as "cloud ear," "wood ear," or simply "edible black fungus." Soak for 20 minutes before using, during which time the mushrooms will expand considerably.
   To choose: Look for dark, well-dried mushrooms.
   To store: Store in an airtight container in a dry place.
   Substitute: Dried *shiitake* mushrooms.

Cucumbers (Kyuri)
Japanese cucumbers are about half the size of Western cucumbers. Their skins are softer and their lower water content makes them crunchier.
   To choose: Look for the smallest, firmest cucumbers.
   Substitute: Half a Western cucumber for every Japanese cucumber.

Peel off the skin and remove any seeds.

Daikon*

Literally "big root," this large white radish finds its way into many Japanese dishes, whether cooked, raw or pickled. Milder than most radishes, it contains enzymes which are said to aid digestion and is served with such foods as Tempura to counteract the oiliness.

To choose: Look for firm, unwrinkled daikon.

To store: Kept in the refrigerator it will last for 1–2 weeks in winter.

See also Momiji-oroshi.

Daikon Sprouts (Kaiware-na)*

These tiny sprouts measuring 2"–3" (5–8 cm) are from the daikon plant. Easy to grow, they are used as a garnish in salads, sashimi and soups for their color and their slightly peppery flavor.

To store: Refrigerate, leaving the base and roots on until needed.

See also Daikon.

Enoki Mushrooms (Enokidake)*

With their long thin white stems and tiny caps, these mushrooms resemble long beansprouts. They have a mild flavor and are used more for their color and texture.

To choose: Look for the whitest mushrooms.

To store: Wrapped in plastic and refrigerated, they will last 1 or 2 days.

Fu*

Fu is made from wheat gluten and formed into decorative shapes. Ume-fu, for instance, is colored and shaped like an ume plum blossom. High in protein and low in starch, it is used mainly in soups, noodle dishes and nabe (one-pot) dishes.

Available fresh or baked. Baked fu must be softened for 5–10 minutes in tepid water before using.

To store: Keep baked fu in an airtight container. Fresh should be frozen to keep.

Ginger (Shoga)*

Japanese cuisine uses only fresh root ginger, never the powdered variety. It is used both as an ingredient in cooked dishes and as a condiment. Ginger stems and various pickled gingers, such as umezu-zuke and sudori-shoga, are also used.

To choose: Look for a firm, unwrinkled ginger root.

To store: Wrapped in plastic and refrigerated, ginger will last for up to 2–3 weeks. It can also be frozen.

Gingko Nuts (Ginnan)*

These delicate nuts have to be cracked open, boiled and have their inner brown skins rubbed off. The bittersweet flavor and the color of the nuts make the effort worth while, and they are attractive additions to such dishes as Harvest Rice.

To store: Fresh nuts will keep for several weeks in the refrigerator.

Grilled Tofu (Yaki-dofu)

Used in Sukiyaki and other nabe dishes. To make, pat dry "cotton" tofu and broil under direct heat until speckled with brown.

See also Tofu.

Harusame*

Meaning "spring showers," these cellophane noodles are made from potatoes, unlike firmer Chinese ones which are made from beans. Soak in lukewarm water for 10 minutes or until soft, then cook until transparent. Rinse. Add at the last minute to soups or nabe (one-pot) dishes.

Substitute: Any other vermicellis.

Kamaboko*

Kamaboko is a term for a wide variety of high-protein fish "sausages." Consisting of white fish pureed, molded and sometimes tinted, they are either steamed or broiled. Can be eaten cold and dipped in shoyu or heated through in clear soups.

To store: Wrapped in plastic and refrigerated, kamaboko will keep for 1 week.

Kampyo*

Another ingredient unique to Japanese cuisine, kampyo consists of dried creamy-colored strips of gourd (cucurbitaceous calabash). They are used either as a filling, as in sushi, or as a decorative and edible tie, as in Eggs in Tofu-Puff Purses. To use, rinse in water, then knead with salt to soften. Boil for a few minutes, or until soft.

To choose: Look for the palest kampyo as it is the freshest.

To store: Keep in an airtight container in a dry place.

Kinome*

The fragrant young leaves of the prickly ash tree, kinome is a springtime garnish. It is used for both its bright green color and its fresh, slightly minty flavor.

To store: Wrapped in plastic and refrigerated, it will last up to 1 week.

Komatsu-na*

Komatsu-na is a leafy green vegetable belonging to the rape family. With its slender stalks and dark leaves, it looks very similar to Japanese spinach.

To store: Wrapped in plastic and refrigerated, komatsu-na will last a couple of days.

To store: Refrigerate wrapped in plastic.

Substitute: Bok choy.

Kombu*

Together with bonito flakes, *kombu* is used to make the dashi stock essential to many Japanese dishes. Do not wash or rinse *kombu*. Wipe only lightly with a cloth, leaving the white powdery coating which is the most flavorful part.

To choose: Look for thick *kombu* with a dark greenish-brown color and a light dusting of white powder on the surface.

To store: Keep in an airtight container in a dry place.

Konnyaku*

Available in both unrefined brown and bleached white, blocks and threads, *konnyaku* is made from the starchy root of the devil's tongue. It is used for its texture—like a very firm jelly—rather than its neutral flavor. It has no calories but is a good source of fiber. Parboil and refresh it in cold water before using.

To store: Cover with water and refrigerate. If the water is changed every day, it will keep for up to 2 weeks.

See also Shirataki.

Kuchinashi-no-mi

Kuchinashi no mi is the dried fruit of the gardenia. When soaked, it releases a natural yellow food coloring.

Lotus Root (Renkon)*

The tubular hollows running through the lotus root make it a very attractive vegetable when sliced. It is used mostly for its decorative effect and crunchy texture in such dishes as Tempura and Kimpira. To prevent it from discoloring after after being cut, soak it in water with a dash of vinegar.

To choose: Look for firm unblemished roots.

To store: Keep in a cool, dark place.

Matcha Green Tea Powder

Also known as *hikicha*, this is a powder made from the buds of the tea plant. It is used both as a flavoring and, as here, as a coloring. The best-quality *matcha* is mixed with hot water and drunk at the traditional tea ceremony. Do not try to grind ordinary green tea leaves, however.

Me-negi*

These slender stalks are *negi* shoots and are used to garnish clear soups.

Mitsuba*

Sometimes known as "Japanese parsley," *mitsuba* is a trefoil with long white stalks. Used for its light color and delicate flavor, *mitsuba* is only blanched before using. It is good in soups, salads and *nabe* (one-pot) dishes.

To store: Covered in plastic and refrigerated, it will keep for up to 1 week.

Mi-zansho no tsukudani

Mi-zansho no Tsukudani is the fruit of the prickly ash simmered in shoyu.

See Sansho and Kinome.

Mustard (Karashi)

Japanese mustard looks similar to some Western mustards but there is a significant difference. It is neither sweet nor vinegary, and, unlike American mustard, it is hot. Available in both powder and paste form, powdered *karashi* is superior. Leave to stand for 10 minutes after mixing, but do not mix too far in advance.

To store: Keep mustard powder in an airtight container in the refrigerator and it will last for 3 or 4 months.

Substitute: Any mustard which is not vinegary or sweet.

Momiji-oroshi

Momiji-oroshi is grated *daikon* to which chilli peppers have been added. To make *momiji-oroshi*, press whole chilli peppers into a piece of *daikon*. Wait a while for the chilli peppers to soften, then grate the *daikon* and drain lightly. A simpler version is to mix commercial chilli powder into grated *daikon* which has been lightly drained.

Myoga Shoots*

Myoga is a shoot belonging to the ginger family, but with an inedible root. Unique to Japanese cuisine, it is often used as an aromatic garnish because of its distinctive flavor and slight hotness.

Negi*

This member of the leek family has slim white stems up to 1" (2.5 cm) thick and 11" (30 cm) long. It is sweeter than the Western leek.

Neri-an

A purée of unsweeted adzuki beans frequently used in Japanese confectionery. If commercially unavailable, it can be easily made at home. To make, boil 1 lb. (450 g) washed adzuki beans in 6 cups water for 40–60 minutes, or until soft. Drain in a cloth-lined colander. Gather up the ends of the cloth and squeeze out the excess water. Blend in a food processor until smooth. Add 1¾–2 cups sugar and a dash of salt and cook over medium heat, stirring with a wooden spoon until well blended. Turn up the heat and cook for a final 10 seconds, or until the paste is thick. Remove from heat and let cool.

Nori*

A dark purplish-green crispy seaweed, *nori* provides the wafer-thin wrappers for the popular sushi rolls. It is available in different shapes and sizes, from large squares to fine shreds. Before using, toast lightly over an open flame or for 2–3 minutes in a moderately hot oven to bring out the flavor.

To choose: Look for a glossy dark *nori*.

To store: Store in an airtight container in a dry place.

Sansho

Although not a member of the peppercorn family, *sansho* is often referred to as "Japanese pepper" because it is spicy, aromatic and resembles peppercorns in appearance. In fact it is the dried pod of the prickly ash, also the source of *kinome*. *Sansho* is used to add a warm spicy note and to counteract the fattiness and strong flavors of meat such as lamb.

To store: In an airtight container, it will keep for up to 1 year.

Seri*

Small green leafy stems with a distinctive flavor and aroma, *seri* is used in *nabe* dishes or served as a side salad in a sesame dressing.

Shichimi-togarashi

A popular seasoning for dishes ranging from Chicken and Leek Kebabs to soups and noodles. Literally meaning "seven-spice pepper," it consists of seven spices from a range of red pepper, black hemp seeds or white poppy seeds, dried tangerine peel, *nori* or *shiso*, *sansho* and sesame seeds.

To store: In an airtight container, it will keep for up to 1 year.

Shiitake Mushrooms (Shiitake)*

Shiitake are prized for their rich woody flavor and aroma which become even more intense when dried. The stems tend to be tough and are usually removed. Soak dried *shiitake* in lukewarm water for 3–5 hours before using, reserving the soaking water for a rich stock.

To choose: Look for fresh mushrooms with a firm brown cap that curls under. When choosing dried ones, look for brown caps with a cracked appearance.

Substitute: Field mushrooms can be used instead of fresh *shiitake*. If they are to be chopped up, dried *shiitake* can be used interchangeably with fresh ones.

To store: Fresh *shiitake* will last for 2 or 3 days if wrapped in plastic and refrigerated. Dried *shiitake* will last indefinitely if kept in an airtight container.

Shimeji Mushrooms (Shimeji)*

A variety of small brown mushrooms are sold under the name *shimeji*. They grown in clumps and are mild in flavor. Good in salads, soups and *nabe* dishes.

To choose: Look for a light brown fleshy caps and thick white stems.

To store: Wrap in plastic and refrigerate for up to 2 or 3 days.

Substitute: Field mushrooms.

Shirataki

Meaning "white waterfalls," *shirataki* is a form of *konnyaku* made into long white threads. Both its "bite" and its ability to absorb the rich sauce make it a delicious addition to Sukiyaki.

To store: As for *konnyaku*.

See also Konnyaku.

Shiratamako*

Shiratamako is a refined flour made from glutinous rice. It is used in confectionery and desserts, such as Fruit Salad with Silky Rice Drops.

Shishi-togarashi Peppers (Shishi-togarashi)*

Despite its appearance, the *shishi-togarashi* is a sweet green chilli pepper that is not hot at all. About 2"–3" (5–8 cm) in length, it needs only to be broiled or deep-fried briefly and makes an attractive garnish.

To choose: Look for firm peppers with a bright color.

To store: Keep in the refrigerator.

Substitute: Slice green peppers into long strips.

Shiso (Ao-jiso)*

A relative of the mint and basil family, the *shiso* leaf has a refreshing almost antiseptic flavor and is rich in calcium and iron. Used mainly as a garnish or condiment, especially in the summer, it may also be used as a vegetable in Tempura. Use whole or finely shredded.

To store: Store in the refrigerator.

Shiso Seed Pods (Hana-ho-jiso)*

These are stems of flowering *shiso* seed pods. They are also used as a garnish for sashimi. Strip the pods from the stem and add to the dish of sashimi dipping sauce.

To store: Stand in water or wrap in a damp paper towel and refrigerate.

Shiso Sprouts (Me-jiso)*

These tiny sprouts are used as a garnish for sashimi.

To store: Stand in water or wrap in a damp paper towel and refrigerate.

Shungiku*

Also known as *kiku-na*, *shungiku* is a leafy green vegetable belonging to the chrysanthemum family. Its slight astringency makes it an interesting addition to *nabe* dishes like Sukiyaki or to salads. Use only the leafy sprigs, not the tough stem.

To choose: Look for young stems without buds or flowers.

To store: Refrigerate wrapped in plastic.

See also Yellow Chrysanthemum Flowers.

Sudachi*

Sudachi is a sharp citrus fruit only about 1" (3 cm) in diameter. Its juice may be used, or the whole fruit may serve as a small container, as in Salmon Roe in Citrus Cups.

Substitute: Lemons or limes.

Sweet Potatoes (Satsuma-imo)*

Literally "potatoes from Satsuma," the Japanese sweet potato originally came from Okinawa via Satsuma. It is slightly sweeter than its American relative and is often used in Japanese confectionery.

To choose: Look for firm unblemished sweet potatoes.

To store: Keep in a cool, dry place.

Tofu (Tofu)

The perfect health food, tofu is packed with protein but low in calories and with absolutely no cholesterol. Made from dried soy beans, it has a subtle flavor and comes in a variety of shapes and forms. The three main kinds are firm (*momen*), "silken" (*kinu*) and *aburage* (deep-fried).

Firm "cotton" tofu has a firm texture and a rough surface. It is used in nabe dishes, such as Sukiyaki. "Silken" tofu, as its name suggests, has a much lighter, smoother texture. It will not withstand much cooking and is therefore used raw, as in Chilled Tofu, or added at the last minute to Miso Soup.

To store: Keep both types under water in the refrigerator. If the water is replaced every day, tofu will keep for up to 2 days.

See also Grilled Tofu and Aburage.

Udo*

Udo is a root vegetable with a distinctive fennel-like fragrance and crisp texture. It is cooked only briefly, sliced thinly and used in soups. Since it is very pungent, however, a lot of the outer flesh is peeled off and the remainder is soaked in vinegar and water before using.

To store: Does not keep well.

Udon Noodles (Udon)*

Available in fresh, pre-cooked and dried forms, these noodles are made from wheat flour. They are paler, softer and thicker than spaghetti.

To store: Refrigerate fresh *udon* wrapped in plastic for up to 3 days. Dried *udon* keep indefinitely.

Substitute: Any thick noodles or pasta, such as fettucine.

Umeboshi

The dried and salted fruit of the *ume* (Japanese plum), *umeboshi* are extremely tart. They are reputed to be good for the digestive system. They also act as a natural preservative, hence their use as a filling for Rice Balls (*Onigiri*).

To store: Stored in a cool dark place, *umeboshi* keep indefinitely.

Wakame*

High in calcium and with a smooth crunchiness, *wakame* makes an excellent addition to salads and cooked dishes, such as Chicken Meatballs with Turnips. Dried *wakame* should be soaked for 20 minutes, blanched in boiling water and refreshed in cold water. Take care not to overcook *wakame*.

To choose: Look for *wakame* with a dark color.

To store: Store in an airtight container in a dry place.

Wakegi*

Wakegi is a member of the leek family but is milder and more tender than the larger leek.

Substitute: Green onions.

See also Asatsuki.

Wasabi*

Often referred to incorrectly as "Japanese horseradish," *wasabi* shares only the same stinging hotness as horseradish. Made from grated *wasabi* root, it is served as a green paste together with sashimi or sandwiched in sushi. It is most widely available in powdered and paste form. When using powdered *wasabi*, allow the paste to stand for 10 minutes before using, but do not make too far in advance as it will lose its flavor.

To store: Keep powdered *wasabi* in an airtight container and *wasabi* paste in the refrigerator. Will last indefinitely.

Yellow Chrysanthemum Flowers*

Whole flowers make a colorful garnish for sashimi. The petals can be marinaded and served raw, as in Shoyu-Steeped Spinach.

To store: Keep refrigerated.

Yuba*

This directly flavored product is made from layer upon layer of the skin which forms on top of soy milk as it is simmered. Available fresh or dried. Soak dried *yuba* in water to soften before using.

Yuzu Citron (Yuzu)*

Different from any other citrus fruit, the *yuzu* is used mainly for its fragrant low peel which serves a garnish in cold seasons.

To store: Refrigerate wrapped in plastic, it will last for 7-10 days.

Substitute: Lemons or limes.

INDEX

ACKNOWLEDGMENTS

Photography	Takehiko Takei
Editor	Michiko Kinoshita
Assisted by	Hiro Tega
Book Design by	Momoyo Nishimura
Sumi Painting by	Rempo Ikeda
Translated by	Keiko Ito
Finished Text by	Jane Singer
	Catherine Meech
Stylist	Emi Fukumoto

Thanks to the following companies for lending tableware.

Yamada Heiando
G2F Hirusaido Terasu
18-12, Sarugaku-cho, Shibuya-ku, Tokyo
Tel: 03-3464-5541
Fax: 03-3464-5543

Tosai
8-8-9, Ginza, Chuo-ku, Tokyo
Tel: 03-3572-1035
Fax: 03-3572-1054

Tokodo
3-21-12, Akasaka, Minato-ku, Tokyo
Tel: 03-3583-3915
Fax: 03-3583-3116

Champêtre
SF Yamachu Annex
6-5-39, Minami Aoyama, Minato-ku, Tokyo
Tel. & Fax: 03-3498-1944

Savoir Vivre
3F, Axis Building, 5-17-1, Roppongi, Minato-ku, Tokyo
Tel: 03-3585-7365
Fax: 03-3582-4705

Daimonji
5-48-3, Jingumae, Shibuya-ku, Tokyo
Tel: 03-3406-7381
Fax: 03-3406-7598